T0346622

# 101 *Fish*

## *A Fly Fisher's Life List*

LEFTY KREH

Illustrations by Bill Bishop

STACKPOLE
BOOKS

Guilford, Connecticut

Published by Stackpole Books
An imprint of The Rowman & Littlefield Publishing Group, Inc.
4501 Forbes Blvd., Ste. 200
Lanham, MD 20706
www.rowman.com

Distributed by NATIONAL BOOK NETWORK

First Stackpole Books paperback edition 2020

British Library Cataloguing in Publication Information available

**Library of Congress Cataloging-in-Publication Data available**

ISBN 978-0-8117-3890-3 (paper : alk. paper)
ISBN 978-0-8117-4846-9 (electronic)

♾™ The paper used in this publication meets the minimum requirements of American National Standard for Information Sciences—Permanence of Paper for Printed Library Materials, ANSI/NISO Z39.48-1992.

# Contents

# Editor's Note

During one of our visits, I asked Lefty if he would be interested in writing a book about all the fish that he has caught on a fly. I had once read that he caught over 80 species on the Clouser Deep Minnow alone and got to thinking that there were very few, if any, people who have caught as many different species of fish as Lefty Kreh—both on fly and conventional tackle. Having already heard him tell some of the stories during our time together over the years, I couldn't help but think that a collection of them written by a man who has fished everywhere from Papua New Guinea to the Florida backcountry would make for a fascinating read.

I suggested that the stories did not have to be about the biggest catches—and he has had plenty of them, having at one time 16 world records—but about the catches that were most memorable to him. After thinking a bit, he agreed to it, and before I left, he looked at me and asked, with a mixture of slight bewilderment and curiosity, "Do you think anyone would want to read a book like this?"

This humility always catches me off-guard, even though it's part of what makes Lefty, Lefty. One of my favorite stories that Lefty tells on himself is of meeting his 5-year-old great-granddaughter in Florida for the first time: "My granddaughter Hillary said, 'Honey, this is your great-grandfather.' Little Alex tilted her head back, looked up at me quizzically, and asked, 'What's so great about him?'"

Ask any fly fisher what is so great about him (besides being able to cast a knife-edge loop a country mile—with either arm) and they might mention the following: he can teach you to fly-cast in half an hour; he created a fly, the Lefty's Deceiver, that is so iconic it graces a postage stamp; he has authored over a dozen books, edited the 25-volume Lefty's Little Library, written countless magazine articles, and is featured in over a dozen videos; and for his lifetime of teaching and fundamental role in developing tackle and techniques for the sport he is honored in the National Fresh Water Fishing Hall of Fame, Fly Fishing Hall of Fame, and IGFA Hall of Fame. Just recently, I read that they named a trail after him along the Gunpowder River in his home state of Maryland.

But, as Ed Jaworowski writes in a recent article in *Fly Fishing in Salt Waters*, "There's far more to his reputation than this impressive output, more than the number and sizes of fish caught, the world records held, the contests won, the awards received and other such accomplishments." *101 Fish* is an engaging record of a remarkable man's fishing trips around the world—Lefty's best cast ever for tarpon, twin Atlantic salmon on two successive casts that both weighed an amazing 37 pounds, Niugini black bass so strong you have to pull them from the brush with a boat—but it is also a collection of stories that reveal the character of a man who deeply values the people met, sights seen, and experiences shared through a lifetime of fishing.

Lefty just wrote the fish stories as they came to him, and the editor in me was tempted to rearrange and organize the text in some orderly fashion. I thought about grouping all the exotic fish—machaca, pacu, barramundi, jacunda—together. Perhaps I would group the rough fish—common carp, yellow sucker, bowfin, bluegill—in case fly fishers not interested in them could go right to the glamour species—the trout, Atlantic salmon, and tarpon. I briefly thought of organizing the book by time period—the early years in Frederick, Maryland; the Miami period when he managed the MET, the largest fishing tournament in the world; his years writing for the *Baltimore Sun*; retirement, which Ev, his wife and best friend of over 65 years, famously quipped that he "flunked."

But better sense prevailed and I more or less left the stories as Lefty wrote them—yellow sucker after tarpon, grass carp after grayling, permit after perch. Their unlikely and often-surprising order reveals a man with a broad love of the outdoors and the camaraderie of an equally wide range of fishing partners, from regular Joes to the rich and famous. I should also note that it was my idea to add genus and species information, just so fly fishers might be able to track down information on some of the exotic fish that are even at the edges of Google's grasp, and any inaccuracies are my fault alone. Lefty prefers to use the common names, which are indeed more colorful.

I hope you enjoy these stories as much as I have.

—*Jay Nichols*

# Tarpon

*Megalops atlanticus,*
silver king, sabalo

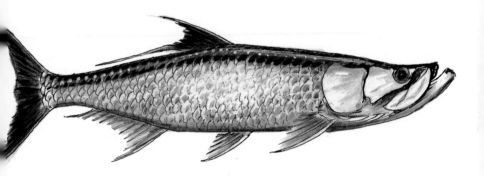

Tarpon are one of the most exciting fish to catch. What is particularly exciting to me is that most of the time we see the fish before we deliver the fly or lure to them. What a thrill it is to watch a giant open its maw and suck in your offering knowing as soon as you set the hook it will rocket upward, throwing water like a broken fire hose.

I have been lucky to catch tarpon on the open ocean and in the roiled jungle rivers of Costa Rica where once a huge bull shark bit in half an 80-pounder right at the boat—awesome and scary. In Cuba not long ago our guide anchored our skiff just outside of some mangroves that had flooded at high tide. Wading to the far side he began to carefully stride through the tangled mangroves in our direction. Suddenly a dozen tarpon of maybe 15 to 20 pounds, seemingly unconcerned, swam into the shallow clear water in front of us. Dropping a fly in front of one, you were rewarded with an instant strike. On a light 8-weight rod this was pure joy.

On a short crushed limestone coral road at Flamingo, a marina base deep in the Everglades, there is a canal best traversed with a canoe as you maneuver under the overhanging mangroves, often filled with mosquitoes that I think were sent out by the Red Cross to get our blood. Once you leave the overhanging trees, there is some open water, and during the 1960s dozens of tiny tarpon from a foot to 18 inches would roll to the surface of the dark water. (They may still be there.) Using tiny popping bugs or small streamers you could have a ball hooking many of these jumping jacks with a 3- or 4-weight fly rod.

But when I think of tarpon, I often remember it was a tarpon that let me make what I believe was my best cast.

About 1968 my son Larry was poling our skiff during a high tide around a small mangrove island near the Content Keys. The tarpon were cruising in and out among the flooded mangrove roots. Larry quietly poled around the end of a tiny island. Before us was a deep indentation in the island's shape forming a small cove.

I had just cast to a 30-pound tarpon at about 50 feet, but it spooked and fled. Then we saw another tarpon slowly meander out from under the roots. It was only about 30 feet away, and I had extended my cast to 50 feet. I lifted the line quietly from the water, and while the line was unrolling on the backcast I stripped in some. As the forward cast unrolled, I continued to recover more line. The cast dropped the fly 30 feet away and three feet in front of the tarpon, who instantly took it.

Even though this fish weighed less than 30 pounds, of all the tarpon I've missed or caught this is my most memorable one. I have often during a cast shot line to obtain more distance. But I had never tried to shorten that much line during the cast.

# Yellow Sucker

2

*Catostomus* sp.,
smooth scale

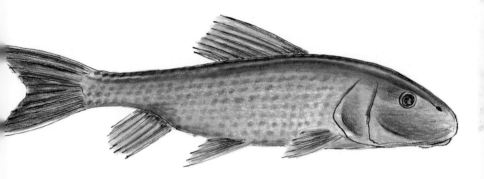

I lived in central Maryland for most of my first 30 some years. It was here that I started fly fishing not long after World War II ended in 1945. For the first several years I fished exclusively for smallmouth bass, generally from our family's Potomac River summer cabin in Lander, Maryland.

The river was alive with smallmouths. I knew almost nothing about fly fishing, but with popping bugs and the crude streamers I learned to tie from a Herter's fly-tying manual, I was able to catch many smallmouths—even 4-pounders.

I knew only one old man, Sam Gardner, who dapped his flies in little Fishing Creek, which tumbled down the Blue Ridge Mountain not far from my home. I really couldn't consider Sam a fly fisherman because the stream he fished averaged less than 20 feet wide. There simply were no other fly fishermen in the counties nearby.

The Chesapeake Bay separates Maryland into Eastern and Western Shores. At the time there was no Bay Bridge so the Eastern Shore was pretty much isolated from the rest of Maryland. But once you were there, the many abandoned, ancient millponds held numbers of big largemouth bass. It was here where I met several fly fishermen who lived in Baltimore. I was elated to be able to talk to someone who also enjoyed fly fishing.

One of these was Tom McNally, who became the outdoor editor for the *Baltimore Sun* newspaper. Together we did a great deal of hunting and fishing. At that time Maryland was lightly populated. The rivers, small streams, and Chesapeake Bay were loaded with fish, and upland game and waterfowl were everywhere.

Tom was also a trout fisherman, and he got me enthused about it. I began to fish drys and wet flies for trout in our local limestone and mountain streams. One day Tom said we should try nymph fishing—something he was just getting interested in.

After he described the type of stream he wanted to fish, I thought I knew the place. My hometown of Frederick is now the second-largest city in Maryland, and excessive development and overpopulation have drawn the water table down so far that many of the streams we fished have disappeared.

I took Tom to Owens Creek, which meanders at the foot of our local Blue Ridge Mountains. Today it is a trickle, but back then it was a fine trout stream. Tom explained that he would show me how to take trout with nymphs.

He showed me his nymph patterns, and we crawled to the base of a pool where we could see trout apparently grabbing nymphs off the bottom. After several futile casts, Tom set the hook, and the fish tore to the upper end of the relatively long pool. Minutes later Tom landed the fish.

We were stunned. It was a husky yellow sucker. At the time, neither of us knew suckers ate nymphs. With Tom's coaching, I soon caught several too. I have since caught many trout on nymphs, but often smile when I think it was yellow suckers that first taught me the trade.

# Northern Pike

# 3

*Esox lucius,*
pike, jackfish, slough shark, gator

There are two kinds of northern pike fishing. Fishing in extreme northern Canada or parts of Alaska is one kind; all other northern pike fishing is different. In most of the United States and Canada, pike have been fished over for years, and it's rare to catch one larger than 10 pounds.

In northern Canada and Alaska, you are fishing where virtually no one lives, and the environment belongs to Mother Nature and her fish and creatures. This area is a true wilderness.

My favorite place is North Seal River Lodge, which has exclusive rights to fish a huge area of northern Manitoba. Fish here for a week—even with flights from the lodges to distant and remote lakes—and you will see no one but the lodge's guests.

What you will see is wilderness, with eagles sweeping down to pick up 20-inch pike and carrying them away to a nest to feed their young. I once heard a wolf howling and tried to imitate the howl. Suddenly 100 yards away a huge gray wolf stepped out on the clear shoreline. He looked at me for a moment with what seemed like disgust and then turned, disappearing in the bush.

The shore lunches are fabulous. You catch char, northern pike, and lake trout from frigid, clear lake waters. The fish are cleaned and within the hour are prepared in a huge, blackened frying pan along with crisp potatoes. It's a meal in that clean, fresh air that rivals the best restaurants in New York City. This is a wild, remote area, and I have never seen a grizzly, but there are many black bears. Some outdoorsmen don't consider black bears to be dangerous, but if their cubs are endangered or they sense you have food and they are frustrated or denied it, they can be very dangerous.

We had just begun enjoying the fried fish and potatoes when we saw a large black bear fast approaching from a nearby sandy hill. There was no doubt it was going to join or take our lunch. The guide grabbed our gear and said quietly, "Let's get the hell out of here."

As one we dashed to our boat, and the guide pushed it 50 yards off the beach where we watched the bear eat everything in sight. It was no problem, though: We soon caught more fish, and the guide prepared another lunch at another location.

As you cruise the lakes in a boat, you will note what appears to be cleared power line swaths similar to those in the United States, but they aren't for power lines. They are paths made by millions of caribou that over the centuries have trodden both north and south on these same paths, giving mature vegetation no chance to grow. The paths lead down to lake edges and then reappear on the far shores—the marches are made when the lakes are covered with ice.

While I have caught many pike weighing more than 20 pounds, perhaps the most interesting northern I caught was with a good fly-fishing friend, Simon Goldseker. Using lead-core shooting heads, we were having fun catching both walleyes and pike in a channel between two islands on a fly-out lake from North Seal River Lodge. I got a strike and soon realized it was a dandy northern, and almost immediately after that Simon hooked a good one. We both fought our fish for several tough minutes. At the same time we both managed to bring our fish to the boat where the guide became excited. A big pike rolled up with my fly and Simon's in its mouth. The greedy pike had taken mine and then grabbed Simon's—a first for both of us.

# Grayling

# 4

*Thymallus thymallus, T. arcticus,*
queen of the waters, arctic trout

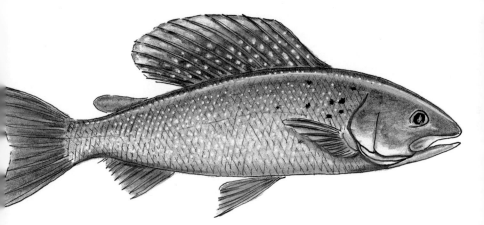

There are a number of grayling species. I've caught the small Montana grayling while fishing some of the mountain streams out west. I also caught grayling in the chalkstreams of both France and England and found them often to be more difficult to deceive with a fly than resident trout. The biggest grayling I've caught have been either in Alaska or in far northern Saskatchewan or Manitoba.

But the most interesting grayling fish I have enjoyed was in Austria. In the early 1950s I wrote an outdoor column for *The County* newspaper in Towson, Maryland, just north of Baltimore. Fen Keyser, who would become one of my best friends, owned the paper. Fen was also a world traveler. My job writing the column was not high-paying, but once a year Fen would take me on a great fishing or hunting trip.

My reward one year was a trip to Europe where we fished trout streams in several countries. I had read about but at the time had not caught the European grayling and mentioned this to Fen, who said he would make that possible.

We drove through the steep and beautiful Austrian mountains to the small town of Bad Ischl, where Fen met with an old friend, Gen. Arthur McChrystal, who after serving in World War II decided to live in Bad Ischl. His home was yards from a river called the Traun. The Traun is wide with fast current as it races down the mountains.

Fen explained to the general that I wanted to catch a grayling, and the general assigned me a local guide whose name I have forgotten. The next morning the guide appeared wearing those leather shorts (lederhosen) and off we went.

I think it is necessary to explain that the only people who fished this area were well-to-do gentlemen who were apparently not too skilled at fly fishing. I noticed that along the riverbank every 40 yards or so were openings where all trees and brush had been cleared—apparently to make fly casting easy for them.

I soon caught my first grayling, a fish with a dorsal fin not unlike that of a miniature sailfish. Releasing the fish, I noted that my hand smelled like the herb thyme, and the guide said that locally they often called it the thyme fish. After fishing two or three of the cleared openings and not getting many strikes, I carefully waded along the shore, avoiding those openings—it was like a bonanza. Apparently the fish holding away from the openings had not seen many flies. I caught a number of grayling and husky brown trout that were darker in color than I have seen before or since.

Unknown to me, the guide recorded each fish and the species as I hooked and landed them. He turned his notes over to General McChrystal, who checked a ledger and with a wide grin said I had set a new record for the most grayling and trout caught in a day.

I am sure the new record was because I did not fish in the "gentlemen's openings." What I was so pleased about was I had finally caught my first grayling in Europe.

# Grass Carp

# 5

*Ctenopharyngodon idella,*
white amur

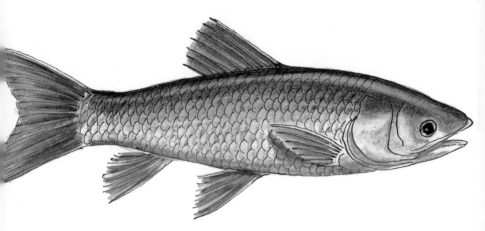

Steve Kantner is well known in South Florida as the "Land Captain" because he guides his clients, by car or canoe, to the myriad canals and often-unknown ponds in the Everglades. If there are fish swimming in the water in his region, Steve knows where they live. Steve is, let's say, active. He is a 220-volt guy living in a 110-volt world—and is pure fun to fish with.

He and his wife Vicki had arranged a seminar for me and promised me some unusual fly fishing if I could stay a day after the seminar. The next morning after breakfast in downtown Fort Lauderdale Steve drove the car along one of the city's busiest streets. We pulled into a parking lot and Steve assembled a 4-weight fly rod. Cars, trucks, and joggers sped by. I was mystified and couldn't imagine where we would fly-fish.

Avoiding traffic, we crossed the main street and in front of us was a deep canal maybe 80 feet wide. Overhanging the water on the far shore were large ficus trees laden with quarter-inch round fruit containing seeds. Steve suggested I strip off a lot of fly line while he tied a quarter-inch cork ball that he had tinted green, matching the color of the ficus seeds.

Then we waited, and I asked why. "I am waiting for the breeze to pick up," Steve answered. Soon a breeze rippled through the ficus trees, and tiny ripe seeds began falling to the water. Within minutes grass carp, some of them almost 20 pounds, began sipping the seeds from the surface.

Steve didn't have to tell me to cast. I threw the tiny cork ball under the overhanging tree and was told not to move it. Less than a minute later I saw a grass carp suck in Steve's ball and I set the hook. The first carp landed was maybe 12 pounds. Larger ones came later and Steve and I had a great time catching big grass carp on a busy street in Fort Lauderdale—maybe the most unique place I ever hooked and landed a fish on a fly rod.

The following year I was traveling to Miami, and a few days before I left I was informed by the airlines that there was a scheduling problem and I would be returning in the afternoon a day later than planned. I called Steve since we had so much fun with those canal grass carp but could not get in touch.

I loaded my travel bag with a fly rod and spinning outfit and a hookless rubber teardrop–shaped casting plug used in casting tournaments. I wasn't sure the idea would work but had high hopes. After my Miami stay the next day I drove to Fort Lauderdale to Steve's location. Both outfits were rigged. It was dead calm. I deliberately cast the hookless rubber plug into the dense branches of a ficus tree overhanging the far side of the canal and began twitching the lure as I retrieved it. The branches began to shake gently, so causing a shower of ficus seeds to fall to the calm canal surface. I quickly retrieved the lure and picked up the fly rod.

Within minutes there were a number of carp sipping the tiny round green seeds, and I cast the cork ball Steve had developed. It lay perfectly still on the water. Soon a good carp inhaled the ball and the rod bent. I spent several hours playing carp under three different ficus trees. Driving to the airport, I couldn't help smiling knowing it wasn't necessary to wait for a breeze to chum carp with ficus berries.

# Rock Bass

# 6

*Ambloplites rupestris,*
redeye bass, goggle eye

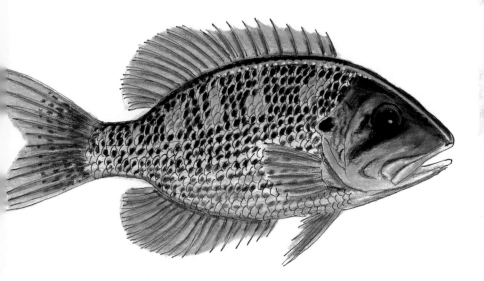

I enjoy catching all kinds of fish—and on all kinds of light tackle. I have never been interested in world records, but I did catch and enter 12 world records after a client who was paying me for promoting fly-fishing many years ago criticized me for throwing back a world record while fishing with him. After 12 records I figured if that isn't enough, the heck with it.

One of my boyhood and lifelong friends is Paul Crum—I grew up with him and we spent many days fishing in central Maryland. Paul and I loved to use 4-weight fly rods or tiny ultra-light spinning rods and 4-pound-test lines to toss 2-inch gold-colored Rapala lures or small Mepps spinners while wading the small streams meandering through our county. We were like kids when we caught sunfish, some smallmouths, and my personal favorite, the rock bass. A good rock bass is a bit larger than a man's hand. They are built like a sunfish or bluegill but have the color of a smallmouth bass. I think they outfight a bluegill once hooked.

A number of times while driving the back roads of my county I crossed a bridge over a ravine, and one day I realized there may be a creek down there. This was many years ago before Google Earth. But I had county topographical maps and used mine to locate a road leading to that mystery stream.

I began wading and fishing with a 4-weight rod and small popping bugs. I caught bluegills and several smallmouths, none more than 12 inches, but the creek seemed filled with husky and aggressive rock bass. I was alone on a summer day having a great time.

After wading upstream for more than an hour I felt the creek's water temperature begin to cool. As I moved farther upstream, the right side seemed to become increasingly cooler. Rounding a sharp bend, I saw why.

On the right, clear, cold water poured into the creek from a limestone spring. I was curious and left the mystery creek to check on this new source. After following the stream and walking about a hundred yards through the woods, I entered a meadow. Walking along and looking in the crystal-clear water, I saw brook trout and some brown trout scurrying to cover. The stream was obviously on a large farm, for I could see no buildings or roads. A limestone stream comes from deep within the earth, and the water temperature remains year-round about fifty degrees for quite some time after it reaches the surface.

A few days later, I fished this stream again and caught native wild brook trout, some close to 12 inches, and fooled a few brown trout. Over the years, I fished it a number of times and never saw anyone. Normally I shared my fishing places with my friends, but this one I selfishly kept for myself. And I owed its discovery to the rock bass.

# Atlantic Salmon

# 7

*Salmo salar,*
grilse, kelt

I was lucky to start at the very top when I first fished for Atlantic salmon. Capt. Bill Curtis was guiding on Biscayne Bay near Miami when he hailed me and my son Larry as we passed by in our boat. He asked me if I would give his client a fly-casting lesson so he could get to the bonefish. I did, and it was how I met and became good friends with Sir James Pearman of Bermuda.

In 1987 Sir James invited me to be his guest for a week on the Spey River in Scotland, and following that, a week of Atlantic salmon on the famed Alta River in Norway. He flew me to and from England on the Concorde.

The week at Ballindalloch Castle was fun, but I had heard so much about the Alta—supposedly the greatest salmon river in the world—that I was eager to get to Norway. I was not to be disappointed.

The Alta is located above the Arctic Circle and is a huge river with many pools deeper than 70 feet. Almost all salmon caught are larger than 20 pounds. The week we were there, Lady Ann Pearman boated one exceeding forty pounds, and one of Sir James's other guests caught one weighing 52 pounds! The farmers who control the valley the Alta runs through insist that all salmon caught be killed and weighed. They use this as a barometer to manage the river. This is hard to believe, but anyone who checks those farmers' records can verify that in one week the six of us caught 106 pounds short of a ton of Atlantic salmon.

This was my first experience using two-handed fly rods, but it was necessary since some of the flies we cast were tied on 6/0 to 10/0 hooks, and on the forward cast if they came close, it sounded like a large bird passing by. This near to the Arctic Circle in June it never gets really dark at night, so we fished from 8 p.m. to 4 a.m., the darkest portion of the day. During the day we slept well since the shutters on the bedroom windows didn't let in sunlight.

As astounding as our total catch was, for me the highlight of the trip was one particular night. We had the lower beat on the river, and the salmon entering it were fresh from the ocean. I was casting a huge 6/0 fly on my 14-foot rod and got a serious strike. The river was deep and the current rapid. The salmon was powerful—no doubt about it—and I thanked the years I had fought saltwater species. I finally got it near the bank, and my guide netted a 37-pounder. The fly was in good shape, so I made another cast and immediately hooked up and a stiff battle ensued. My guide finally netted the second great salmon, which turned out be another 37-pounder. I had caught, on two successive casts, the two largest Atlantic salmon I have ever caught—thanks to the Alta River.

# Oscar

*Astronotus ocellatus,*
velvet cichlid, tiger oscar

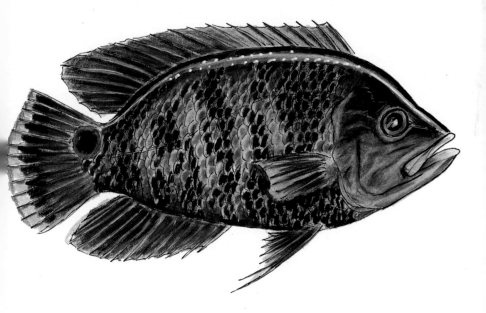

When I moved to Florida in 1964 with my family, I realized the Everglades was less than half a mile from my new home. My son Larry and I prowled the "River of Grass" fishing with fly, plug, and spin tackle—me mostly using a fly.

Our first trips were along the Tamiami Trail, where a canal borders the road running from Miami west to the coast, terminating at Naples, Florida. There were lots of small tarpon and largemouth bass, and the waters teemed with all types of panfish from bluegills to stump knockers (a species of sunfish).

By taking almost abandoned dirt roads that penetrated this vast, watery swamp, we located many canals few others fished and caught even bigger fish than we did along the Tamiami Trail. I had an 8-weight fly rod and Larry used 12-pound-test spinning gear for the big snook we sought. But most of the time I simply enjoyed fishing with a light 4- or 5-weight fly rod for the baby tarpon and small snook, but the best fun was with the uncountable numbers of panfish. I thought a 1-pound bluegill was an incredible fighter and often said that if they grew much bigger it would take strong tackle to land them.

Recently—not long before this writing—I had a seminar on the west coast of Florida. While at the seminar I found that my flight the next morning had been canceled and I couldn't leave until that evening. I borrowed a 4-weight fly rod outfit and drove to some Everglades canals I had fished years ago, intending to battle some of those tough bluegills.

I quickly caught a lot of fish—but no bluegills. The canals were filled with all sorts of aquarium fish that people had apparently dumped there. I was a bit disappointed until I began using a small Clouser Minnow with a white belly and chartreuse top. I got a serious strike that I assumed was from a large bass. When the fight ended I landed a fish about 13 inches long, but I didn't know what it was. I had never seen a fish like it. The mouth was upturned like a tarpon and seemed unusually large for the size of the fish. Most of the body was a medium green with strange, jagged, orange markings zigzagging across its sides.

Back home I found it was an oscar, a tropical fish. I would describe it as 13 inches of fish muscle surrounded by fins. The strong bluegill took a backseat to this critter. As I drove to the airport I realized I had just caught the hardest-fighting fish I ever landed on a 4-weight rod.

# Snook

*Centropomus undecimalis,*
robalo, lineside

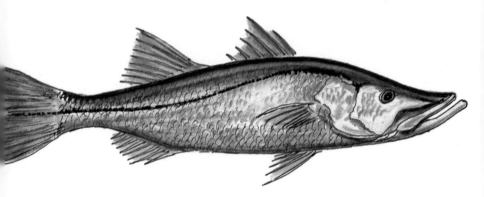

I n 1960 I traveled to Belize, a Central American country where people speak English. To my knowledge at that time there were maybe three or four fishing lodges in the entire country. I was lucky I would be fishing at a new one on the Turneffe Islands, located 30 miles offshore to the east. The Turneffes are mainly clusters of mangroves, but here and there is enough solid land to be called a true island. The Turneffes are maybe 30 miles long and sit on the edge of the second-largest barrier reef in the world.

I had caught a number of snook on fly but never more than 24 inches. At a seminar I met two guys who claimed if I went to the just-opened Turneffe Island Lodge located on the island group's extreme southern tip I would surely get a snook better than two feet long.

After crossing 30 miles of open water in a slow-moving old boat, I arrived at the lodge. The owner, Vic Barothy, who ran a fishing camp on Pine Island in Cuba and had to escape when Fidel Castro took over, met me. Vic assigned me to a native guide named Phillip, who was maybe 5 feet, 2 inches tall and weighed 140 pounds. We got along famously.

I won't bore you with the thousands of bonefish we saw and the uncounted numbers we caught. On the second day I told Phillip I really came to catch a big snook, and he said we could do that in the morning. There was a soft knock on my bedroom door well before dawn that awakened me to see Phillip standing in the doorway.

I dressed quickly and we stole quietly out of the lodge. The evening before he had me rig my fly rod with a large white Deceiver with a gray top attached to a 40-pound shock leader. He cautioned me to be silent as we got into the boat, and he poled us no more than 150 yards from the lodge. He pointed and I cast to a drop-off sandbar near the mangroves. I started a retrieve and got a jolting strike and hooked and landed a 42-inch snook—still my best on the fly. But for me the best was yet to come.

I made arrangements to come back the following year and requested Phillip again as my guide. When I arrived, Phillip greeted me. The next morning we were off for bonefish. We sat in the anchored boat eating our lunch while Phillip told me one of the most interesting stories I've heard in all my years of fishing.

When not guiding, Phillip used his sailboat for commercial fishing. He said that he and his son were in the Turneffes fishing and did not realize a hurricane was approaching. By the time they did it was too late. They did what all natives do—they ran their boat well up into a mangrove creek, where the tough trees furnish the best shelter from the storm.

After securely tying the boat, they waited out the hurricane. At the peak of the storm, because of the storm surge, the boat sank, and they stood chest deep in the water for hours.

After the storm it took several days to get the boat in shape and to sail home. Landing at the Belize City Docks, they tied up the boat and walked up the street toward their home. On the way they were met by a funeral procession formed by Phillip's wife. Seeing her husband and her son walking toward her, Phillip said his wife fainted away in the street.

A remarkable story that to me was better than my big snook.

# Saratoga

# 10

*Scleropages* sp.

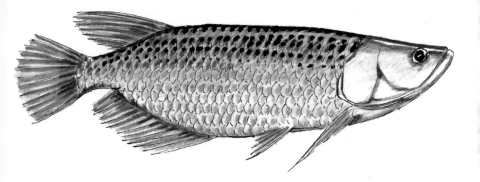

I n 1987 I made my first fishing trip to Australia. I can't explain how excited I was to be there. Rod Harrison (everyone over there calls him Harro) is the senior outdoor writer in the country. He wrote asking if would I be interested in coming over "for a fish." I didn't write—I immediately called by phone.

It took 24 agonizing hours to get there, and in my anxious mind it seemed like three days. When I arrived at the airport, Rod stepped forward to meet me. He was surprisingly short but stout. I thought, "I hope he is a friendly guy"—no one could be more so. We quickly became best friends and even today as I write this we are e-mailing back and forth.

The next few years I made several trips with Rod; some were for making TV shows but some just for fishing fun. During one trip we flew to Darwin, overnighted, and the next morning in a small plane went north to Barra Base Fishing Lodge on Bathurst Island. Bathurst Island is located offshore northeast of the mainland. I believe the lodge was the only habitation on the huge island excepting some Aborigines.

Graeme and Dorothee Williams ran the lodge. It was situated on an inlet from the sea. The lodge was very comfortable, with air-conditioned rooms and good basic foods including plenty of fresh tropical fruits.

There was a wide beach that dropped off rather sharply to deeper water filled with saltwater crocodiles. When we first arrived, there were about 15 dogs that would come down and bark at the crocs. Two years later, I returned and realized the dogs were slow learners, for there were no dogs left.

Each evening one of the Australians would wade out hip deep with the remains of the fish the cook had filleted for our meal. Soon a huge grouper, maybe 200 or more pounds, would appear and be hand-fed the fish—an awesome sight. They had named the grouper Oscar.

I was very much interested in catching a saratoga, a prehistoric fish that some said had been around a million years. Its head somewhat resembles a tarpon with the same underslung jaw. It lived in freshwater rivers.

We made a long boat trip over the choppy sea to Melville Island, one of the largest and most remote islands in the country. We anchored the boat near the mouth of Goose Creek, said to hold a mother lode of saratogas. Just off the river mouth was a sandy island with a few trees where we camped for the night. We caught some fish and cooked them over an open fire, and as we ate we were rewarded with a spectacular sunset.

We sat beside the fire chatting and listening to a pack of dingo dogs chasing their prey. Silently and seemingly out of nowhere appeared several Aborigines with spears. The Australians welcomed them and offered some of the fish we caught that had not been cooked. They immediately gutted the fish and to my dismay placed them on the low-burning coals, turning them over every several minutes. I had never seen fish cooked in that manner—I expected the coals to burn them. Instead one of the Aborigines lifted the fish off the coals and offered me some. The flesh was moist and delicious.

The next morning we ran up Goose Creek, a small, winding river on Melville Island with no sign of human habitation. I was told that saratogas hit surface stuff, so I had an ample supply of Dahlberg Divers and popping bugs. The fish hang out around lily pads, and the river was choked in places with them.

Rod Harrison suggested chucking one back into a hole in the pads and popping the bug twice. I did as ordered, and a strange-looking fish appeared. I loved fishing with a popping bug for saratogas. They reminded me of slow-witted bass. As I made a cast, the bug popped once or twice and a saratoga would appear inches below the bug. What was so much fun is after the fish had been drawn to the noisy bug it would not strike until you moved the bug. I found it fun to wait as long as I could before moving the bug for the strike.

The largest average saratoga we caught was maybe 3 or 4 pounds, but on a light 6-weight rod they were fun. The highlight of the trip was a monster saratoga that Rod caught—everyone said they had never seen one that big.

# Redfish

*Sciaenops ocellatus,*
red drum, channel bass, red

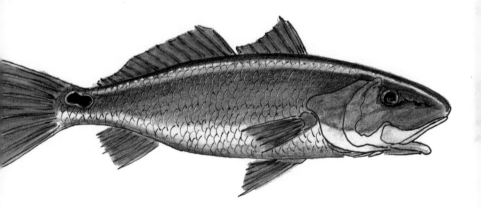

I've been lucky to catch redfish on a fly in many places, and my best is just less than 30 pounds. My favorite place is the marshes of Louisiana, where the fishing is certainly the best ever—and the people are great. Yet my most memorable red fishing trip was not because I caught redfish but what we saw.

For a number of years four of us—Ken Whellams from Calgary, Canada, and Flip Pallot and Ted Juracsik from Florida, and myself—would meet at Ted's fishing camp on Chokoloskee Bay at the north end of Florida's Ten Thousand Islands.

One day Ted poled our skiff silently into a still, back cove of the Everglades. Ted, Ken, and I were looking for redfish with rods ready to cast. We noticed some "nervous water" just ahead. Ted inched the boat ahead. Ted had spent decades in the Everglades penetrating places few ever see. I certainly spent a number of years in the Glades, but we were now treated to a sight few other than maybe some of the old Seminole Indians may have witnessed.

Reaching the rippled water, we saw a huge manatee with a newborn, I guess you might call a calf. The tiny manatee was about the diameter of a loaf of bread and perhaps 22 inches long—and as black as a moonless night.

The mother was teaching it to swim. She positioned the front portion of her head under the baby's body and rapidly flipped her head sideways, which would shoot the baby through the water. At first the tiny manatee just shot forward and then began to sink. The mother would quickly move under it and repositioned the baby, repeating the process.

Ken, Ted, and I were fascinated. We are not sure how long we watched the patient mother, but after a considerable time, the baby began to move its paddle-like back fin and soon after it was swimming. We all wanted to clap and cheer for the mother.

All of us have spent our lives in the outdoors, but we agreed this treat we came across when seeking redfish was one of the most unique sights we ever saw.

# Jack Crevalle

*Caranx hippos,*
jack, crevally

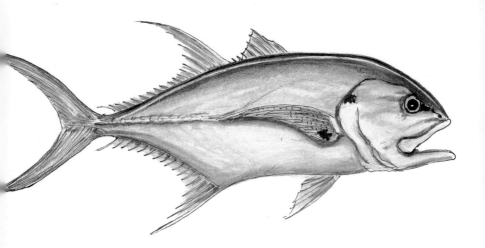

During the mid-1960s in Miami, I managed what at the time was the largest fishing tournament in the world: in 16 weeks we received more than 200,000 entries. Started in 1929, the tournament's missions were twofold: One was to promote the angling industry of South Florida; it's hard to believe today, but the second mission was to encourage people to move there. One of my jobs was to take writers from the North who, it was hoped, would go home and write glowing accounts of the fishing, enticing their readers to come south and enjoy the sport.

The jack crevalle is a fish with an oval-shaped body and a sickle tail. It has a bad temper, is all muscle, and best of all I never knew a jack that wasn't hungry. Throw something at it and it fought you for it. It was the perfect "tourist fish."

Many, many times tourist writers would hook a jack and exclaim over and over about how hard it fought. They'd hook a second jack and give another

**23**

glowing account, saying what a hard-fighting, wonderful fish it was. But when they hooked the third fish, the now worn-out anglers would almost always say, "Another damn jack." I tell you this so you will understand that for its size, it is one of the toughest fish you can catch on light tackle.

In the mid-1960s Capt. Gene Montgomery and I were in his 19-foot boat near Cosgrove Light west of Key West. The seas were rough and we were bouncing around. We saw some fish breaking and I inadvertently picked up the wrong fly rod. It was an 8-weight fiberglass rod equipped with a Scientific Anglers freshwater reel that had no drag, just a click to keep the spool from over-running. The tippet was a fragile 6-pound-test.

I made a cast, a big jack grabbed the Deceiver fly, and I realized I was in trouble. I needed a bigger rod and certainly a reel with a saltwater drag and most of all a stronger tippet. But it was too late. I fought the fish for maybe 20 minutes and twice got it near the boat.

Then the worst thing happened. The reel loosened and fell from the rod. As I tried to grab the reel, the jack would take line and the revolving spool caused it to jump around the boat's deck. It was like trying to catch a cornered rat. Realizing the problem, Gene yelled, "Hold on." I grabbed the side of the boat, and he surged forward, creating a lot of slack line. I snatched the reel from the deck and quickly reattached it to the rod.

We eventually landed the jack crevalle. It weighed 19 pounds, 4 ounces, and for many years stood as the 6-pound class tippet fly rod world record.

Considering the tackle, the fish being fought, and the conditions, I regard it as the best catch I've made on a fly rod, although I have taken many far larger fish.

# Seatrout

13

*Cynoscion nebulosus,*
spotted seatrout, speckled trout, speck,
trout, spotted weakfish

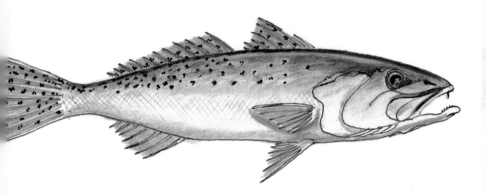

About 1958, Tom Cofield, a good friend and the outdoor editor for the *Baltimore News-American* newspaper, suggested we go to Florida to fish. We both saved some money, and driving Tom's car, bid our wives farewell. I was off to my first great fishing adventure.

There were no interstates or superhighways in those days, so we drove south on US 1. The highway, if you want to call it that, was clogged with tiny towns, stoplights, some scary bridges, and bad stretches of road, and before we returned to Maryland, we had used the two spare tires.

In Georgia there were a lot of poor people who didn't have enough money to buy mosquito underwear. The towns were hard up, so they figured out how to get traveling tourists to augment their local coffers. We were only in the state a short time before Tom and I made our "donation."

Here's how it worked: US 1 had a speed limit of 45 to 50 mph. (Remember, this was not an interstate.) We were traveling the speed limit when we would come upon a sign that indicated a city limit—50 yards later the speed limit was 25 mph and 50 yards beyond that sat the local law—often a pot-bellied officer who obviously had eaten too much fried chicken. Before we could get the car slowed from 45 to 25 mph the officer had us in as neat a speed trap as you could imagine. Being fast learners, whenever we saw buildings or a distant sign we slowed and were only caught once.

We planned to fish from northern Florida down to the Keys. When we got to Jacksonville, we thought we were almost to the Keys only to find we were a little more than halfway from Maryland to our final destination.

*Field and Stream* magazine conducted a fishing contest, and every year the largest seatrout were caught in the Indian or Banana rivers, so we made that a prime stop.

At a nearby fishing and bait shop, we asked how and where to fish for the trout. The owner, when he determined we weren't going to buy anything, was about as friendly as an alarm clock. Outside sat a nice old-timer who was friendly and gave us the info we sought.

Apparently the best fishing was at night, so we had a late dinner and began wading the shallows as directed, casting all-white Deceivers. Suddenly I felt a tug and Tom yelled that he did too. It was so dark we couldn't see each other, and we fought our fish for a few minutes until the two outdoor writers finally figured out we had hooked each other's lines and were not fighting a fish. After a good laugh we fished until nearly midnight and caught several nice seatrout in the 4- to 6-pound size.

I told Tom I needed to shower and go to bed and was going take one last cast. I began the retrieve and got a strike. It was obviously a bigger fish of some kind than we had previously landed.

When I finally lifted it from the water we weighed it on an accurate spring scale, and it tipped in at 9 pounds—a real trophy. After photographing and putting it back we waded ashore. I never caught another seatrout that big.

# Barjack

# 14

*Carangoides ruber,*
skipjack, reef runner, Bahama runner, carbonero,
red jack, blue-striped cavalla, passing jack

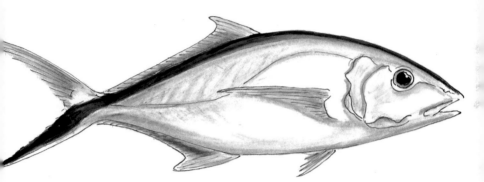

L iving in South Florida during the mid-1960s was almost like being near an aquarium filled with wild fish. The Everglades were less than an hour away, and myriad deep, clean canals with largemouth bass and sunfish meandered everywhere. Biscayne Bay was at our doorstep, and minutes from it was the Atlantic Ocean and the Gulf Stream. Yep, this was fisherman's paradise.

In the summer months the Gulf Stream was a few miles from shore. It was then that my son Larry and I would chase barjack. They are one of the many species of jacks roaming the tropical seas, easily distinguished from other jacks by the dark horizontal black bar extending along their backs and into the lower portion of their tails. Any fish with a sickle-shaped tail will be a problem when hooked, and barjacks have that tail.

If winds blew steadily from the east for two or three days during the hot summer, they would push huge floating masses of aquatic grasses along the edge of the Gulf Stream, flowing north like a big river. Baby fish born in the ocean hid among the dense floating weeds, as did crabs and shrimp. Barjacks knew this, and when large masses of the floating grasses accumulated along the edge of the Gulf Stream, Larry and I would head out in our 16-foot aluminum boat.

What fun we had. The sea would be oily, slick, and calm, and by motoring slowly along the edge of the weedlines, we could cast to schools of marauding barjacks. Because of the weeds, we often cast weedless Bendback patterns, but the most fun was to throw popping bugs and see these jack tear into them. You could hardly have more fun with an 8-weight rod.

Barjacks are not good eating, so this was catch-and-release. But occasionally small to medium-size dolphin would also join the jacks, and a few of them would come home for the table.

# Archerfish

# 15

## *Toxotes chatareus*

In 1987 I was lucky to spend several weeks fishing in Australia's outback, the Arafura Sea to the north, and the remote Bathurst and Melville islands. We first spent time in the Kimberly region, a vast, barren outback sparsely peopled here and there with Aborigines.

We were flown there by floatplane and landed on a remote river called the Drysdale. A comfortable "camp" had been set up for us. It consisted of some wooden benches, a table, and individual mosquito-net tents (there was no fear of rain) and at night weird creatures visited us.

That first night was fabulous. As the sun started down, a fire was built and we had a barbie (what we would call a grill) and I could smell the steaks cooking. I don't drink, and so I had a coke while the others had something obviously a bit stronger. Just at dusk there was a strange noise and thousands of fruit bats from a close-by rookery flew overhead. These bats are huge—I'd judge their wingspan to be more than 4 feet and they probably weighed

2 pounds. They offered no danger to us since their main food is fruit, but it was an inspiring sight each evening when they came over our campsite like dark clouds.

Our camp was just below a falls on the river, which was about 250 yards wide. Saltwater crocodiles had been protected since 1972 and had completely lost their fear of man. I arose before anyone the first morning. It was calm and the water was like a sheet of oiled glass. Lying 150 yards out from the bank was the largest croc I ever saw. The others guessed it might be 17 or 18 feet long.

Later that morning one of the fellows hung a dead barramundi (similar to our snook) about 4 feet above the water on a stout limb. "Watch the bloody bastard," he urged, so we sat motionless. Hardly seeming to move, the croc slowly approached the suspended barra. Suddenly, it used its giant tail to push the huge body upward, and it lunged at the barra. I swear the belly was at least 4 feet wide, and I have no idea how much this monster croc weighed. Closing its huge jaws around the barra, it easily snapped the limb and disappeared beneath the surface with the fish and limb. It was the greatest exhibition of raw natural power I ever saw.

After breakfast I sat on the bank where some small trees overhung the water. Suddenly I saw a stream of water emit from the surface and then a fish swirled. After the third such event I realized I was watching an archerfish. They somewhat resemble our panfish, and I noticed an insect on a limb close to the water. Then like a small water pistol, the fish shot an accurate stream of water, knocking the insect to the water, and ate it.

I tied on a small bonefish fly and teased it in front of several archerfish and caught one that was perhaps 12 inches long. The fellows told me it was the largest archerfish they had seen caught. It was the first of many species I landed on a fly rod in Australia.

# Giant Needlefish 16

*Tylosurus crocodilus,*
needlefish, long tom, houndfish

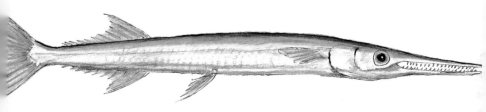

Anyone who has spent much time in saltwater has seen a needlefish. There are about 50 species, and the ones most commonly seen are as thin as a cigar, about 12 to 18 inches long, and bear the silvery sides and green back similar to most of the species. All needlefish have a long, thin jaw armed with needle-like teeth. A 10- to 14-inch hose lure with a hook or two attached is undoubtedly the most effective barracuda lure ever. It can be retrieved rapidly underwater or across the surface imitating a needlefish running on the surface with only the lower body in the water. 'Cudas love to eat needlefish.

I have caught needlefish of many sizes, but the one most interesting for me is what Bahamians call a long tom. This species is anywhere from 3 to a little more than 4 feet in length.

Often, when startled by a fast-moving boat, they will speed across the water above the surface propelled by their tails or leap high. When living in Florida I read in one of our papers about a native from Bimini in the Bahamas running his boat at night. A startled long tom leaped above the surface and the long, thin beak was impaled in the native's chest, killing him upon impact.

Long toms are fun to catch on a lure or fly—but there are two problems in successfully landing them. Because of their long, thin, bony mouth filled with sharp teeth, it is difficult to impale a hook on the strike. Even worse, no fish you ever caught is so acrobatic. The moment a long tom feels the hook, it is above water rapidly undulating its long, thin body attempting to throw the hook. They go through such gyrations that sometimes the body bends enough so that the beak touches the tail, completing a circle.

Needlefish are almost always released. The body is so thin there is little meat even on a large one, and the greenish bones don't present an attractive meal when cooked.

# Piranha

Family Characidae,
piraña, caribe

There are fearsome tales about piranha stripping the meat from a cow wading across a river or fatally attacking people. Natives scoff at such stories. I now tend to believe them.

Simon Goldseker and Don Peters, two fishing buddies and I, flew to the River Plate operation in north central Brazil. It's more sophisticated now, but our camp was situated on a sandy beach and consisted of small individual pup tents with tiny battery-operated fans, supposedly to cool you on a hot jungle night.

When we arrived we were greeted by Ruby, a little Brazilian lady. We were given something to eat, and Simon began casting a small Rattletrap lure in the dark-brown waters washing against the beach. He began hooking a piranha every several casts. I asked Ruby how you take a bath, and she said you put on your swimsuit and wade out with a bar of soap and wash yourself. Don and I immediately asked about the piranhas Simon was catching, and she explained that they don't bother you unless you are bleeding.

"Okay, you do it for us," I said.

She did and nothing happened. The first two days we ventured into the water only ankle deep; after that we enjoyed immersing ourselves in the warm water among piranhas.

Piranhas are really fun to catch on a 4-, 5-, or 6-weight rod. I suggest using a sinking tip or sinking-head fly line, and one of the most effective lures is a small chartreuse and white or chartreuse and yellow Clouser Minnow. This pattern can be tied in a matter of minutes, and the head should be coated with epoxy. If you are lucky, you will get three or four fish before all of the material is gone but what remains under the epoxy. Of course, you need a short, thin wire leader.

There are several dozen varieties of piranhas. Most are about the size of an average bluegill, and the largest I have seen have been the negro or black piranha. On our trip we caught many that weighed 2 pounds.

My biggest surprise concerning piranhas came when the native guides kept for lunch a 3- or 4-pound peacock bass and some black piranhas. We beached the boat at an opening in the jungle, and they built a grill frame of green sticks. Soon they had a fire that had burned down to hot coals. They gutted the fish and placed them on the green-stick grill, turning the fish every so often. To my surprise the piranha tasted like pompano—delicious—making it one of the tastiest shore lunches ever.

# Steelhead

*Oncorhynchus mykiss*,
steelie, chromer, metalhead

I have caught steelhead in Alaskan streams, in Oregon and Washington, and in some of the rivers that empty into our Great Lakes. All of this has been great fun. I had heard often that *the place* to catch steelheads was the Dean River in British Columbia. Many years ago Don Green, owner of Sage Rod Company, invited me to fish the Dean—an invitation he annually shared with several others.

I was impressed even before reaching the river. We flew in a fairly small plane to Bella Coola, a tiny town situated in a deep valley of the same name. We had been flying over snow-capped mountains when the plane began a sudden descent. Well above the mountain peaks, I watched the pilot suddenly aim the plane for the deep valley several thousand feet below. I can tell you my hands were gripping the armrests, but we landed safely.

The Dean is a big, brawling river and a historic steelhead destination. We fished it by wading and making long casts under the eyes of topflight guides. My biggest steelhead had been a 15-pounder, and on the first day with a wet fly I landed my largest of the trip, a 22-pounder. I was pumped. The next day I caught my biggest on a dry fly, a 16-pounder—still today my best two steel-heads. Anyone who loves steelheading should try to get on the Dean.

But for me the trip was a sad one. There were only two camps on the river. As I write this I am 87 and my memory for names is not what it used to be, but I think the other camp owner's first name was Bud. He used a small helicopter to ferry his clients to good fishing spots along the river. Each day we would see him flying low and waving at us as he transported his clients.

Near the end of the trip I was wading out from a gravel bar when Bud flew by in a different helicopter. He was having his serviced and had rented a different one. Later that day we got the terrible news. Bud had landed and dis-charged his clients. For some reason he opened his door and stood up, but the whirling propellers on the helicopter were much lower than on his own and he was instantly killed.

When I think of the Dean River it is with great sadness.

# Narrow-Barred Spanish Mackerel 19

*Scomberomorus commerson*,
nine-barred mackerel, blue mackerel,
barred mackerel, narrow-bar

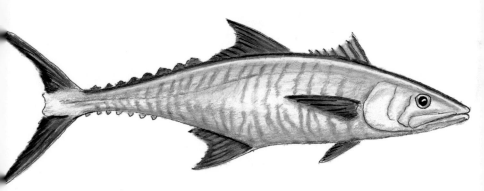

During the late 1980s and early 1990s I made several trips to Australia, arranged by Rod Harrison, the dean of Australian fishing and one of my most cherished friends.

He isn't tall, maybe 5 feet, 9 inches. Built like a bank-vault door, he is almost a third as wide, with biceps larger than my thighs. Most of the time he is a gentle soul. But not always.

Because of a car accident, he was forced to retire from the local police force, but his police companion told me a great story about him from the time when he was on the force. He said they got a call about a guy standing on a hotel bed and using some sort of kung fu to thrash anyone who tried to get him to vacate the room.

Rod's friend stands well over 6 feet and looks like a pro football player. They entered the room and Rod's buddy said he reached for the man and a foot came out of nowhere and he landed stunned against the far wall.

He said Rod marched up to the fellow and attempted to hit him on the chin. The man moved his head sideways and Rod's arm punched through the wall into the next hotel room. The man began kicking Rod in his side. Rod withdrew his bloody arm. Walking around to the bottom of the bed he folded it, pushing the bed against the wall, and trapping the man. He held the bed in that position for about two minutes. They opened the bed, put the cuffs on the prostrate man, and hauled him off to jail.

One of the toughest offshore species I caught on a fly with Rod was the narrow-barred Spanish mackerel, locally often called doggie or kingfish. We located the mackerel easily. Lying beneath a school of prey fish, these long, narrow fish swept upward with such incredible speed that they would rocket out of the water, easily detected by us. My best fish on a fly was perhaps 30 pounds, and having caught wahoo I believe that pound for pound they are just as strong and fast.

But my most memorable moment associated with this species came after we stopped fishing and were heading toward Melville Island for the evening. Following us was another of our charter boats. Luckily I happened to look back and witnessed the highest-jumping fish I had ever seen. A mackerel had skyrocketed out of the water in a huge arc behind the charter boat. The fish jumped higher than the flying bridge on the boat as it soared in a rainbow-shaped loop from one side to the other. I have never again seen any fish make a leap like that.

# Ladyfish

# 20

*Elops* sp.,
ten-pounder, chiro

The ladyfish is found throughout tropical waters and is called by a host of names. I believe the biggest species are off the African coast and might grow to more than 4 feet in length. But most ladyfish anglers' catches weigh maybe a half pound to a pound and a half and are rather small. For their size, they fight like hell. They are extremely acrobatic and have a rough interior mouth, so you need a short bite leader of 20- to 40-pound-test mono if you plan to land them. Flies and jigs are generally tied on hook sizes 1, 2, or 4.

Light spinning gear or 6-weight fly rods are ideal tackle. Small white jigs for spinning and light-colored Clousers work well when searching the waters for them. A favorite pastime of many who spend their winters in South Florida is fishing at night on the upstream tide side around lighted bridges. Another good place to fish for ladyfish at night is a lighted dock. Since docks have ladders, dangling ropes, and other fly-grabbing things, I like to use small bendback-style patterns that are virtually weedless.

For years I never caught a ladyfish weighing more than 2 pounds. That was until in the early 1980s when I fished some inland bays at the Turneffe Islands 30 miles east of Belize. Encountering a school of fish in the shallows harassing bait, we began casting small white flies to the melee. We were stunned to realize we were catching huge ladyfish. I could barely get my hand around their long, sleek bodies, and I am sure that some of them weighed more than 4 pounds. Never before or since have I caught such trophies.

I once asked a guide in the Ten Thousand Islands of Florida why they call them ladyfish. His answer: "You understand a real lady wants to be handled gently. You know, if you squeeze one too hard, it will crap on you." I am not sure that is the right answer.

# Brown Trout

# 21

*Salmo trutta*

I have been fortunate to land brown trout from waters in Europe, all through the United States, much of South America, and New Zealand. But when I think of this grand fish there are two catches that I recall most fondly. Actually one of the catches was made by a friend.

I have fished a number of locations in New Zealand (the best trout fishing anywhere), but my favorite is Cedar Lodge near Cromwell on the South Island. Owner Dick Fraser helicoptered me and longtime fishing buddy Del Brown (who later caught more than 500 saltwater permit on a fly) to a remote river. Dick then left, promising to be back in a few hours.

The New Zealand streams are air-clear, and Del and I had a grand time sighting and taking turns catching browns and rainbows. Crouching while sneaking along a high bank, Del and I saw a big brown feeding on nymphs. We sat down and studied the situation. Every so often the big brown would open its white mouth and suck in another nymph.

This was a perfect place to take some photos. If Del approached from downstream and I shot photos from this high angle on the elevated bank, I could get a nice sequence.

Del got in the water and slowly took a position. Because the fish was deep Del couldn't tell exactly where it was feeding, but I was able to direct his casts from the high bank. On the fifth try his nymph drifted downstream perfectly. The fish took, and ten minutes later Del landed a huge brown of maybe 12 pounds. We were both elated—it was one of his best browns and I got a great sequence of photos.

The other brown I will never forget. Brown trout arrive to spawn in the early fall at Sodus Point, New York, where a small stream flows into Sodus Bay. Unlike the darkly colored browns of rivers and streams, these lake browns are bright silver and could be confused with steelheads.

I was in a belly boat just off the mouth of the small stream casting a seven-weight rod in hopes of hooking into one of these big browns. A fish struck and on the hook set it took off. The leader was 12-pound-test, and it was soon apparent the fish was towing me out into the bay. At first I wasn't concerned, but when I was pulled well past a pier jutting out into the bay, I tried to break the 12-pound-test. When you are in a belly boat you can't break 12-pound-test mono.

The fish towed me several hundred yards out into open water and I didn't know what to do. My only option was to throw away the rod and reel—something I didn't want. I heard a boat approaching and waved frantically. As it neared me I saw in it a young couple. The young lady was wearing a bathing suit you could put in an aspirin box—but this time I took little notice. Luckily they had a wooden platform on the boat's stern and I was able to climb on it and land the fish. I don't know how much it weighed, but it was at least 10 or 12 pounds.

I released the fish and the couple took me back to shore. This was a lesson for me. Never again when fishing in a belly boat for those big browns would I be without a small anchor.

# Jacunda

# 22

*Crenicichla* sp.

I have been fortunate to fish many places on our planet, from the greatest of all Atlantic salmon rivers—the Alta, 100 miles north of the arctic circle—to the southern part of New Zealand not too far from Antarctica, where in my mind is the best trout fishing in the world. Fishing for northern pike in upper Manitoba and Saskatchewan is exciting as much for the pure wildness of the place. There is a certain appeal that is hard to describe when, as a guest of writer and friend John Goddard, flies are cast on the Test and other chalk-streams in England where the sport we love began centuries ago. But of all the places fish have been chased I think the upper Amazon basin has been one of the most interesting. Certainly there is a huge variety of exciting species, but it is pure jungle and fishing there is like sitting in a real-life movie where you see things never witnessed before. Raw nature is constantly surprising anglers. One minute a flock of gorgeous multicolored birds fly overhead and the next you may encounter a strange animal swimming in the river.

Most anglers planning a trip to the northern Amazon basin only think of catching big peacock bass—and that's understandable. It sounds crazy, but I enjoy catching all fish—big or small. One of the things that endeared me to

New Guinea was that on my first trip there in 1987 I landed twenty species new to me. Some of them were only 2 or 3 pounds—but all were exciting and enjoyable. Whenever I take a fishing trip where the quarry is a large, strong species I always take with me a light fly-rod outfit and some small flies. Time and again either the fishing is so good with the bigger species it gets a little boring or that part of the trip is a bust and the lighter tackle enables me to mess around with small stuff that bends the hell out of the rod.

Take along some light fly or spinning tackle for those times when you aren't catching big peacocks. A 6-weight fly rod armed with either a floating or sinking line or a spinning outfit with 6- to 10-pound test can turn a slow day into a fun-filled one.

One of my favorite species to catch on light fly or spinning gear is the jacunda. This is a cichlid family fish that weighs no more than 4 pounds. Long and fairly slender, it has a light belly, dark back, and some orange spots. It is a favorite food of the larger peacock bass, and if was I limited to one Deceiver or Half and Half pattern for peacocks in the region, I would opt for a black and orange fly.

Jacunda feed on small baitfish so streamers, small plugs, or action-tail jigs all work. They can often be seen prowling close to the riverbanks, trapping the small baitfish and then swooping in to gorge on them. I have enjoyed some wonderful hours catching these hard-fighting little critters with light tackle.

Another of the smaller and ignored species of the Amazon basin is the pacu, which is shaped somewhat like our bluegills but can grow considerably larger and has silvery sides and a darker back. I think they are in the same family as the piranha. They have teeth, but they are not as sharp as those of the piranhas, so you need a 4-inch bite leader of thin wire. The average size caught is maybe 1 to 3 pounds, but I was lucky enough to get one that was perhaps 6 pounds—imagine fighting a 6-pound bluegill on a light fly rod.

One reason I like catching pacu is they are excellent table fare. Theodore Roosevelt in his book *Through the Brazilian Wilderness* wrote how he enjoyed catching them on light rods and how good they were to eat.

I've had great sport when visiting some exotic waters when I took a light fly outfit with me and caught ignored species, like the pacu or jacunda.

# Common Carp

# 23

*Cyprinus carpio carpio,*
golden ghost, Rocky Mountain bonefish

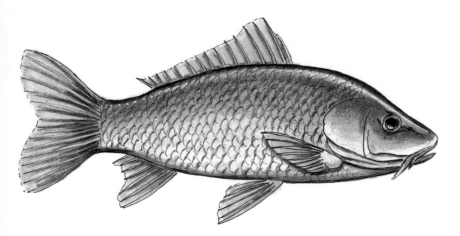

I n the last two decades, fly fishermen have learned that one of the shyest, most difficult fish to catch in fresh water is the carp. A small carp is a 3- or 4-pounder, and in some areas you have a good chance to hook carp weighing more than 20 pounds—and all muscle. Once hooked, a carp is often into the backing as if a saltwater species was on the other end. Long leaders and weight-forward lines with a 10- to 20-foot clear tip offer an advantage.

Carp can be very selective and tend to eat what is available locally. If you fish many of the Western streams, their main food source is pretty much the same as trout—so nymphs are usually best. In the Great Lakes region, crayfish and leeches are prime foods, and a black Woolly Bugger fools many carp. Quarries filled with clear water in Ohio often have mulberry trees overhanging the banks. A mulberry fly pattern that looks like a berry and sinks at the same rate is a must. In southern Florida's canal system, the grass carp feed on ficus berries so a round cork ball tinted green does the trick.

Flip Pallot is one of my best friends, and we have fished over the planet with a fly rod. For many years Flip produced *Walker's Cay Chronicles,* regarded by many as the best fishing TV show ever. Flip often said, "Lefty, if you see a situation that would make a good show, let's do it." I suggested we try the West Branch of the Susquehanna near Williamsport, Pennsylvania, and fish for carp with Mike O'Brien, the local expert. The river is wide and air-clear. The carp in these rivers feed on crayfish, and they will use their heads to turn over stones to flush escaping crayfish.

The method is to pole the boat quietly and look for muds made as the carp disturb the bottom while overturning stones. This usually occurs in water from 1 to 3 feet deep, so it's all visual fishing. The key is to drop the weighted fly in front of the fish as it leaves the mud and then allow it to get to the bottom before retrieving.

The morning we were to begin filming there was a misty rain. We sat around the hotel room drinking coffee and killing time. Finally the film crew decided to go to the river and eat lunch in the van; if the sun came out, we could do some shooting. In the motel room I quickly assembled the 8-weight fly rod and tied on the fly, and we were off. As we arrived at the river the sun came out and there were smiles everywhere. We put the boats in and Mike began poling while Flip and I looked for our first carp.

The camera boat stayed close by. A mudding carp was soon spotted and Mike eased the boat within casting distance. Flip made a perfect presentation, and the carp agreed and was hooked. Flip was soon into the reel's backing. Everything was going fine and the film crew was delighted. Suddenly the line went slack and I was astonished as I asked, "Flip you didn't break that fish off did you?" "I don't think so," he replied.

Reeling in the line, he looked at the leader tippet and then held it close to the camera lens. There was the spiraled pigtail on the end, a sure sign the knot was not closed properly and the carp had pulled free. I hung my head in shame. I always used my pliers to test such a knot after it is tied to be sure it is firmly closed, but in the motel room when I quickly assembled the outfit I didn't have my pliers handy and just held the knot in my fingers to close it. It was a big mistake. Luckily we had no trouble catching enough carp after that for the show.

On the way back that afternoon I moaned about my mistake, and Flip put his arm around me and said, "We won't show that on TV." I replied, "The devil you won't—they love to see people screw up on TV." Flip agreed and many people have since commented on it with a chuckle.

# Lake Trout

# 24

*Salvelinus namaycush,*
lakers, paperbelly, mackinaw, togue

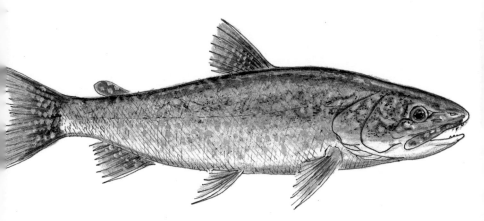

One of the great targets for fly fishermen is the lake trout, but to find quality fishing, you need to travel to the far north of Canada. Saskatchewan and Manitoba are where I have enjoyed catching fish from 5 to 25 pounds on flies.

The problem is that lake trout prefer to live most of the year at coldwater depths to as much as 100 feet. Immediately after the ice melts on the lake's surface, the trout move to the shallow boulder reefs and remain there until the water temperatures inch toward 60 degrees, when the fish slowly descend into the depths.

When on these shallow reefs less than 12 to 15 feet deep, anglers casting streamers that are baitfish imitations with intermediate to fast-sinking shooting heads have the best lake trout fishing. But Mother Nature is not reliable in scheduling ice-out. Often the angler arrives at the lake and it is too early or late and the fish are in the depths.

This happened to me several decades ago when I arrived at Scott Lake in Saskatchewan the last week of June. The guides told me the lake trout had been up on the boulder fields and were now down deep. One of the guides had a good depth finder and he cruised to a known location. On the depth finder I could see layers of trout at 70 to 100 feet.

I had several lead-core shooting heads with me as well as some tying materials. Back at camp I secured ⅛-ounce egg sinkers on the hook shanks immediately behind the hook eyes. I then built some large, flashy flies at least a foot long.

The guide took me back to the site where those layers of trout were down deep. I stripped off the fly and a short 3-foot leader plus the lead-core head and 80 feet of shooting line and allowed it to descend to the layers of trout below. I started a vertical retrieve and on the second drop I connected with a trout of about 8 pounds. During that week perhaps 30 lake trout were taken on that rig. It isn't true fly fishing by some standards, but I had a grand time. Since then many others have enjoyed the same technique, only a bit more refined. Tungsten-coated line sinks faster than lead-core line, for example, and whereas I started using bouyant deer hair, anglers now use synthetics to dress the fly so that it sinks faster.

You never know what trout will grab your fly. My most memorable "almost catch" was at North Seal River Lodge in Manitoba. Working over a layer of trout the depth finder said were at 75 feet, I began a fast vertical retrieve and hooked what I thought was a trout of about 8 pounds. Minutes into the fight the shooting line was torn from my fingers, and after recovering it I began to fight what had to be a big trout. Perhaps 30 feet from the surface the heavy tension suddenly ceased, and I brought to the boat a dead lake trout of about 8 pounds. Across the center of its body were deep impressions from the mouth of a huge trout that attempted to kill and eat it. That's the one I would like to have landed.

# White and
# Black Crappie

# 25

*Pomoxis* spp.,
speck, calico bass, crappie, papermouth

The white or black crappie is a delicious-to-eat panfish. They can be found in lakes and quiet waters across the country. Crappie are members of the sunfish and black bass family and can be identified by their light-colored bellies and prominent black specks. White and black crappie often swim together. On a white crappie, the black specks are arranged in seven to nine distinct vertical bars, whereas black crappie have random blotches.

They are a wonderful fish to catch on a 3- to 5-weight rod and line. Some of my best crappie fishing was at Lake Okeechobee, Florida. A nice crappie in most northern lakes is 10 to 12 inches, but at Lake Okeechobee many can be caught to 18 inches—slabsiders, as the locals call them. Flies dressed on size 8 or 10 hooks with a bit of marabou wing are a killer.

Crappie are school fish, and once you locate them, if you get the right fly to the correct depth, you can catch a number before they wise up. Crappie are unusual in that they tend not to hold near the surface or near the bottom but hover in the mid-depths.

To locate a school, we employed an old trick. With the first crappie caught, we would use a 2-foot length of thin sewing thread with a small hook on one end and a balloon inflated on the other end to the size of a man's thumb. The small hook was impaled in the dorsal fin of the first one caught and the crappie released. It of course swam back to the school. It was simple to cast near the tiny balloon and have our fun. When we were done we recovered our "guide" and freed the fish.

# Machaca

*Brycon* sp.

I have never enjoyed fishing popping bugs more than when fishing for machaca. It requires excellent coordination and lightning-like reflexes. The machaca is a fish that lives in the jungle rivers of Costa Rica. It can reach 6 or 8 pounds but most are smaller. The body is slightly rounded, covered in dark silver scales, and the mouth is filled with small, sharp teeth. One of its favorite foods is a type of seed that falls from trees into the river.

These jungle rivers are usually swift and often discolored since they are constantly eroding their shorelines. Within a foot or so of the banks there is usually calm water where the machaca lie in wait to pounce on anything that passes by.

Small popping bugs dressed on a size 1/0 hook are my favorite. I make the popper as simple as possible and include just a short tail so it will cast properly. After three or four machacas, their teeth have destroyed the bug, so I carry a lot of them.

The Rio Colorado is a big, fast-moving river, and the game plan is for the guide to keep the boat within casting distance of the shoreline and the angler to cast right against the shore. With a rapidly moving boat and an uneven shoreline, this is one of the most challenging popping bug situations ever. The swift current is tearing the boat downstream, you make a cast and pop the bug close to the bank, make a short retrieve and instantly make another cast, repeating this over and over. I call it machine-gun bass bugging and I love it.

# Catfish

*Ictalurus* sp.,
blue catfish, cat

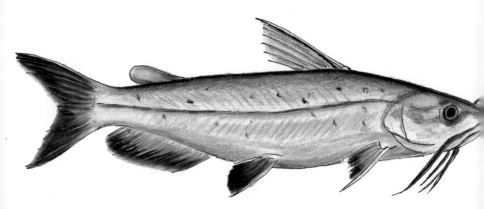

Some years ago a good friend, Gene Mueller, invited me to cover a bass fly-fishing tournament on the Rappahannock River in Virginia. I was outdoor editor of the *Baltimore Sun*, and Gene held the same position with the *Washington Times*. We decided to fish together so we could help each other get material and photos about other contestants.

The Rap is a big river that flows across much of the state and into the Chesapeake Bay. We were fishing below Fredericksburg on the tidal section, a portion of the Rap known for its largemouth fishing. The shorelines are cluttered with washed-up logs, drowned timber, and other bass-holding structure, not to mention the thousands of areas of lily pads—prime habitat for largemouths.

Gene I were doing okay—we had caught several bass in the 2- to 3-pound size, but knew other angles were sure to do better. Gene is great fun to be with, and I recall on a trip to the Ventuari River in Venezuela where Gene held a huge, half-wild baby river otter while I removed a 3/0 hook from its foot pad.

Gene was handling the electric motor since he was more skilled than me. There was a large log half-submerged along the bank with a small water opening behind it. He moved in, and I cast a popping bug into the opening and received an immediate solid strike.

When I set the hook, the 8-weight rod bent dangerously and for several minutes I was unable to move the fish. "We are going to win this tournament," Gene yelled. "That has to be the granddaddy of all bass in this river."

The fish moved away from the log and into the river. With just a 10-pound tippet, I was careful not to apply too much pressure. Ten minutes later we had the fish at the boat. When Gene tried to net it, the net was too small. He lifted it into the boat.

We were both dismayed and astonished. It was huge blue catfish. We didn't weigh it, but it was by far the largest catfish I have landed on a fly rod. And the only catfish I ever had caught on a popping bug.

As the tournament day ended we were not in the running with our catch, but for Gene and me, that big blue catfish made the trip a memorable one.

# Niugini Black Bass

28

*Lutjanus goldiei*,
Papuan black bass, black snapper, black bass

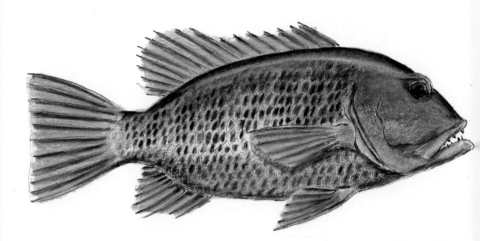

O f all the places on the planet I have fly-fished, my favorite is New Guinea. With the few exceptions of those who live in towns, the rest of the population lives in the jungles much as they did before the time of Christ. The natives still hunt with bows and arrows. There are almost no roads, no television, newspapers, or things the rest of the world considers commonplace. To give you an idea of what life is like there, we were in western New Guinea on the Bensbach River when we met a native whose dugout was filled with watermelons. He seemed friendly, so we asked if we could have several of the melons. His answer told it all: "I'll give you the watermelons if you bring the seeds back." They have no stores.

It was in New Guinea where I met what some regard as the hardest-fighting fish to be caught on a fly, the Niugini black bass.

In 1987 I spent several weeks in Australia and New Guinea with my good friend Rod Harrison. We fished remote islands as well as the outback, sometimes filming TV shows. I quickly learned during those weeks that Aussies love to play jokes or tricks on each other. So when they said we would be going to New Guinea to film catching the Niugini black bass, they told vivid and descriptive stories that this was the strongest, meanest, most ferocious fish you could ever catch on a fly. It is caught near river mouths that empty in the sea. They called the fish "River Rambo." Naturally I thought they were setting me up for a joke.

We arrived by helicopter at the Kulu River. A clearing had been cut in the dense jungle and a thatched hut had just been constructed for us to live in. As I peered down from the descending helicopter, I could see natives with bones in their hair, their bodies painted, holding bows and arrows or spears. They looked as friendly as prison guards, but it turned out they were pleasant.

That first night, Rod asked me to help him load reels with line. They were medium trolling reels for offshore fishing. I helped him put 40-pound-test on one reel and 60-pound-test on the other. Then Rod removed all the treble hooks from his ⅛-inch lures and threw them in the trash. "What's wrong with the hooks?" I asked. "Not strong enough," he answered as he installed heavy-duty ones.

I thought to myself, they are trying to pull another joke on me, so I'll go along with it. I rigged my offshore sailfish fly rod and big reel; the leader was 20-pound-test with a Bimini Twist on each end attached to an 80-pound mono bite leader with a Deceiver pattern dressed on a 5/0 carbon-steel hook. I was armed about as powerful as ever.

When we got in the boat the next morning to run down the Kulu River, I noted that Rod's two outfits were loaded with the 40- and 60-pound mono, and the lures carried the heavy-duty hooks. Wow, I wondered, was he serious about these nasty fish?

The fishing method for the black bass is to locate a tree that has tumbled into the river. The bass tend to hide among the sunken branches and ambush any prey. They dart out, grab the prey, and dive back into the tangled limbs. If the boat can drag the black bass into open water away from the tree and the fly fisherman can keep it there for two minutes, the fish will usually give up.

The boat pulled up to the first sunken tree and our mate Dean Butler put the motor in neutral. Rod told me, "You have a go." Now wary about the situation I answered, "No, you have a go." Rod repeated his request and I again answered, "I ain't going until you go."

Rod stood up, grabbed the 40-pound stout outfit, and used his pliers to lock the drag. He definitely had my attention. Rod is one of the strongest men

I know. He made a cast with the lure alongside the sunken tree and began a retrieve. Out darted a big greenish fish that grabbed the lure. Rod yelled to Dean, "Hit it, Dean," and Dean reversed the motor to back the boat away from the tree while Rod held on for dear life. The rod took a frightful bend and suddenly the 40-pound line broke, making a popping sound like a .22-caliber rifle when fired.

I reached down and began to get rid of that 20-pound tippet on my line. Taking a length of Rod's 40-pound mono, I made a single-strand leader straight from the line to the fly. At the next sunken tree, I wasn't yet ready, so Rod picked up the 50-pound outfit, cast, and when this fish was hooked, it was able to get back into the tree and we finally had to cut the line.

We were making a TV show for the Australian audience. When we arrived at the next sunken tree, I stood with the heaviest fly tackle I had ever cast. The Big Deceiver went alongside the tree and a huge green shape lunged out and grabbed the fly. "Hit it, Dean," and Dean put the motor in reverse and attempted to drag the fish into open water. Instead, the powerful black bass streaked back under the tree branches, creating a rope burn with the fly line clenched tightly in my hand. The TV cameraman later took a closeup of the white friction groove running across my palm. Re-rigged, we came to the next tree and this time I was ready. I cast, started the retrieve, and out lunged the black bass, grabbing my fly. Immediately I struck and wrapped the line around the reel foot two times. "Hit it, Dean," I yelled, and he backed the boat into open water.

Once out in the open river, I unwrapped the line from the reel, and the battle began. I had been told if you can fight one for two minutes, they give up, but it was the damndest two minutes I had experienced with a fly rod. When I finally landed the fish, and they filmed it, the bass weighed only about 14 pounds. I could not believe any fish that size could battle so hard on such heavy tackle.

The second day I landed a black bass estimated to be about 28 pounds. I am here to say that no fish inshore or offshore has ever fought me so hard. At this writing I think maybe less than two dozen people have landed one on a fly rod.

# Bonefish

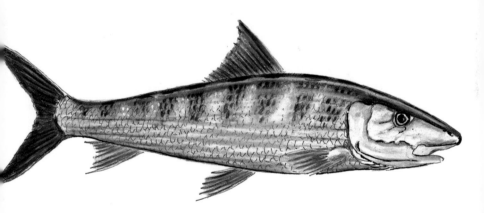

## 29

*Albula* spp.,
gray ghost, bone, white fox, banana fish,
phantom, silver ghost, ladyfish, grubber

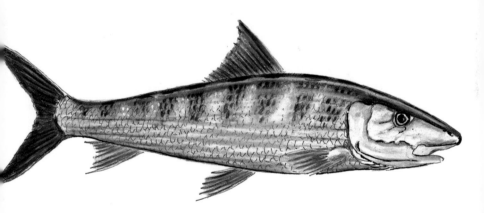

've been lucky to catch more than 100 species of fish on a fly rod, ranging from billfish in the Pacific Ocean to Dolly Varden in Alaska. But if you ask my favorite species to seek with a fly rod, the answer is bonefish.

Bonefish live in some of the clearest water on the planet, so fishing for bonefish is visual fishing. Whether you are wading or seeking them from a boat, you are constantly on the move. There is always activity on a bonefish flat. A blacktip shark may show up, investigating the mud left by the boat pole. Crabs, mantis shrimp, and small species of fish dart away at your approach. A gull, osprey, or pelican may dive, taking its prey, or you may find a ray beneath the bottom, stirring mud to flush its food from beneath.

There is more. You fish for bones with light tackle—a 6-weight rod and line is ideal on calm days, and rarely do you need more than an 8-weight. The fish are so cautious they are like cats in a dog pound, ready to flee at any moment.

Once a bonefish is hooked, it tears line from the reel so fast it's hard to believe that this small fish can be so powerful. But a bonefish fight is over in a short time—no need to use heavy tackle battling a powerful beast. Once at boatside, it can be released, and the whole wonderful process begins anew.

Not one but two events stand out in my mind when I think of the bonefish that God, the guide, and the weather allowed me to land.

When Castro took over Cuba in 1959, my mentor, famed writer Joe Brooks, was hired by Castro to send writers to Cuba to promote sport fishing as a means of Castro generating money to run the new government. Joe selected two others and me to go with him, and we arrived a week or two after the revolution for an 18-day stay. We fished all over Cuba, including Treasure Lake, which was regarded at the time as the best largemouth bass lake in the world—and for that I have no argument.

But the highlight of the trip for me was when we were taken by a huge sailboat to the north coast at what I thought was a place called Cayo Galenda. Anyway, we were going to fish for bonefish—my first chance at them. I had a Pflueger Medalist 1498 freshwater reel with no drag and a 9-weight fiberglass rod Joe had suggested I purchase.

The guide pulled up to a hard coral flat, and we waded no more than 100 yards when he said cast to a silvery tail waving above the surface. The fly dropped beside the fish; when I felt tension I set the hook, and that's when I fell in love with bonefish. Never—and I mean *never*—had a fish pulled so much line and backing from my reel so fast. I was astonished.

The guide kept yelling something in Spanish like "mucho grande," and I had no idea what he was saying. A l-o-n-g ways across the flat I saw a fish flopping in the shallows, and it took a while for me to realize that the distant fish was the one I hooked. We landed my first bonefish, and the guide's scale indicated it weighed 10 pounds. It was a long time before I caught a bigger one.

The other most memorable bonefish event happened with my best friend Irv Swope, with whom I fished around the planet for more than 50 years and never once did we have a cross word.

Capt. Rupert Leadon, who I think has the best eyes for seeing flats fish, is owner of Andros Island Bonefish Club. Years ago, Rupert made a long boat run to the west side of Andros when at that time virtually no one ventured there. The west side is shallow for miles off the island, and we arrived under perfect conditions. There wasn't a cloud in the sky and just enough breeze to put a small ripple on the water but not enough to interfere with seeing the bones.

Rupert was poling in a foot of water perhaps half a mile from shore. Everywhere we looked were bonefish in schools, singles, and doubles. Irv had tied on a tan and white Clouser dressed on a size 2 hook, and I had the same pattern but with a white and chartreuse wing.

It was the greatest day of bonefish Irv or I ever experienced. Almost every cast we made within 10 feet of a bonefish would cause it to surge forward and grab the fly. It was obvious these bones had rarely seen a fly. At lunchtime while we sat on the gunwale of the boat eating, Rupert said to Irv, "There's a bonefish 30 feet away; why don't you try for him." Irv put down his sandwich and while still sitting, picked up his rod, cast, and hooked about a 7-pounder. Before lunch was over, I landed one about as big while sitting on the gunwale on the other side of the boat.

I never keep count of fish, but this day was so spectacular I did. I weighed 24 bonefish that were more than 6 pounds, 4 more than 10 pounds, and Irv landed an 11-pounder—that was not counting the many smaller ones. It was the best day of bonefishing I ever had.

# Brook Trout

30

*Salvelinus fontinalis,*
speckled or spotted trout, brookie,
coaster, squaretail

For a number of years the brook trout I caught were in the Blue Ridge Mountains near my home in Frederick, Maryland. A trophy was 12 or 13 inches, and many were less than 6 inches. All were fun because you had to catch them in narrow, overgrown mountain creeks with short pools and little backcasting room. It was a challenge to deliver the fly accurately and still make a good presentation.

Then I fished in Labrador, where a 13-inch brook trout was a midget. The best fishing I experienced for large brook trout was at Osprey Lake Lodge on a lake of the same name that lies at the head of the Eagle River, well known for its Atlantic salmon fishing. Many years ago the lodge really wasn't a lodge as it is now. It was constructed from fir trees that had been squared with a chain saw. They were put into the ground and sheets of plywood were nailed to them. A tarpaper roof completed the structure, which kept out most weather. But the fishing was worth staying there for.

On my first trip there, my friend and I caught a number of brookies between 4 and 6 pounds with small streamers and dry flies. On my second trip, I witnessed the most intense hatch of huge caddisflies. The monster caddis rained down on the water in incredible numbers, and the brook trout went crazy. Not prepared for casting a large caddis pattern, I switched to a big Royal Wulff, and they ate it. During the hatch, I caught a 9-pound brook trout. I had never seen one that large.

But that was not my most memorable moment brook trout fishing. We were scheduled to return home on a certain day. The weather was horrible—winds 30 to 40 mph and rainsqualls. Our floatplane could not get to us until four days later.

We ran short of food, and on the third day the cook told me bring in trout since we needed something to eat. I caught and killed a 4-pounder and hated it. When I gave it to the cook he said go out and get one a little bigger—this isn't enough. There was a small floating dock in front of our camp. I walked on it, cast a Mickey Finn, and began retrieving. A 6-pound brookie took the fly. I walked back five minutes after departing and casually said, "Is this okay?" He answered, "Yeah, that's fine."

Walking away, I wondered how many places there are where you can walk out on a dock and within minutes catch a 6-pound brook trout—and the cook expected that?

# Giant Trevally

## 31

*Caranx ignobilis,*
GT, great trevally

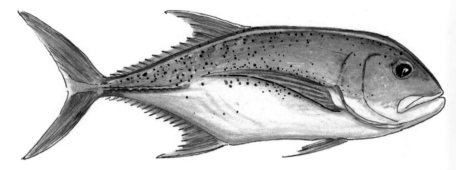

A nglers go to Christmas Island because it is one of the premier bonefishing destinations in the world. The flats—mostly firm with a smooth, hard bottom—are some of the best in the world for the wading angler. You can walk sometimes a mile or more searching for bones. Because the atoll is located almost at the equator, when the sun rises it is almost overhead until late afternoon—giving flats anglers some of the best light conditions for seeing fish almost anywhere.

Among the first fly fishermen to fish this largest of all atolls, we were not aware these flats also held some of the strongest fish in the sea—giant trevally.

There are a number of species of trevally that inhabit a wide range of the Pacific Ocean. Many trevallys rarely reach 10 pounds, but the giant trevally is a true giant and can weigh more than 100 pounds. The trevallys closely resemble in body shape the jack crevalle that inhabits Florida and the Caribbean. Anyone who has caught a jack knows that it is one of the strongest fish for its size—imagine a jack crevalle that weighs 50 or more pounds.

While giant trevallys are often hooked on fly tackle in most places over reefs and wrecks, they are so strong they can dive into the structure and break off. Outdoor writer and superb offshore fly rodder Nick Curcione told me about his trip to Midway Island. Nick brought along a large number of shooting heads, intending to land some giant trevally abundant on the nearby coral reefs. He hooked many, but during the battle the trevallys reached the rocky reefs below, taking with them almost all of Nick's horde of fly lines. But Christmas Island is different. It is the largest atoll in the world and lies in the middle of the Pacific Ocean 1,200 miles south of Honolulu. The entire center of the atoll is made up of flats, small lagoons, and channels. There is an opening in the atoll to the Pacific, and giant trevally use it to get inside and feed on the astounding numbers of bonefish that reside on the flats.

It is here that a fly fisherman has the best chance to catch a giant trevally on a fly. The reason fly fishermen can land these giants at Christmas Island is the lagoons have a soft, almost mushy bottom. During their frantic escape attempt, they pump silt into their gills and slowly lose strength.

The guide carries a 12-weight outfit rigged with either a large popping bug or streamer while the angler carries his bonefish outfit. Should a giant trevally be sighted, the angler switches rods and casts to the giant.

My guide suggested standing at the edge of a deep channel where there was a rather shallow ditch coming from the flat and ending at the channel. The tide was falling, and as the water began to dry the flat, the bonefish headed for safety in the deeper water. Suddenly there appeared what I thought were three 70- to 90-pound tarpon at the mouth of the ditch.

Down the ditch with the falling tide came a school of bonefish, and when they reached the channel, the three monster fish surged forward, grabbing the hapless bones. One leviathan came almost out of the water, and I saw the deep body and realized these were giant trevally I previously had only seen in inshore waters. I badly wanted to hook one, but I was armed with a 7-weight rod and line and could only watch the carnage.

On a later trip my guide and I waded a bonefish flat near a channel. My guide carried a 12-weight rod with a floating line and a large popping bug tied to a short leader that carried a 60-pound-test monofilament bite leader.

I had caught several bonefish when my guide said quietly, "Give me your rod," as he handed me the 12-weight. Slowly coming toward us in less than 4 feet of water was a big trevally. I quickly stripped line off the reel, and with a few false casts, I dropped the big popping bug 10 feet in front of the trevally. One loud pop of the bug and the trevally surged forward. To get the bug in the shallows, it raised a portion of itself above the surface and engulfed the fly. I used my body to help sink the hook deep. The first 75 or so yards of line were gone in seconds, and it was all I could do to hang on. We were in a shallow lagoon, and the fish raced around the lagoon looking for an escape route. I applied as much pressure as I dared. Finally the fish began to tire, and when we landed it, we estimated it to be between 60 and 70 pounds.

# Walleye

*Sander vitreus,*
walleyed pike perch, walleyed pickerel, walleye pike

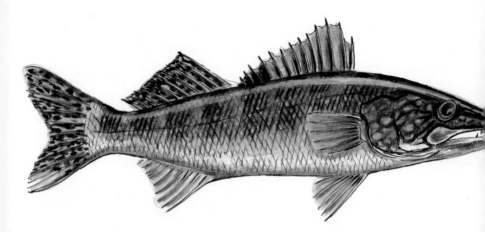

Throughout the upper Midwest, the walleye is one of the most popular of all fish sought by anglers. Anyone looking for a battle on their tackle will be disappointed, for no one ever got a heart attack fighting a walleye. But are they good eating? Many of the most prestigious and finest local restaurants carry walleye on their menus, and for good reason. I regard the walleye as perhaps the tastiest of all of freshwater fish in our country.

Northern Saskatchewan and Manitoba—where I love to catch big northern pike—often have schools of walleyes. If a guide can locate a school of these by using a sinking line and small Clouser Minnow in chartreuse and white or a wing of chartreuse and yellow, you can often catch all the walleyes you want.

During the midday break, the guide prepares a shore lunch. Locating a good spot, the guide builds a fire and cleans the fish. Within minutes after starting, the first gulls start showing up, yet you may not have not seen one for hours. It must be their incredible eyesight that helps them see the fire's smoke.

Few meals are tastier anywhere than a shore lunch of thinly sliced and well-done potatoes and hunks of fried walleyes.

# Morocoto

*Colossoma macropomum*

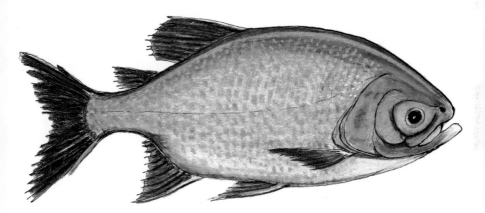

Without a doubt the hardest-fighting fish I ever caught that had the smallest mouth is the morocoto in the Ventura River in extreme western Venezuela near the Colombian border.

It was quite a trip to get to Manaka Lodge. I don't know if the camp is still open since it lies so close to Colombia. Bandits from Colombia raided the camp the week after we left, killed the manager, and plundered the area.

Our guide spoke little English and indicated there was a special fish he called a morocoto we might try to catch on a fly rod. He said he had never heard of anyone catching them on anything but bait and they fought like the devil. After a long upriver run, we came to a quiet pool with a large rock ledge at the bottom.

We cast a number of flies with no success. The guide then put a small piece of bait on a hook and cast it out with a spinning outfit, allowing it to freely drift in the current. Almost immediately there was a strike, and the rod bent dangerously. After a real struggle, he brought to the boat a fish of about 12 pounds. It was dark brown and shaped much like a bluegill. For such a large-bodied fish, it had a tiny mouth filled with teeth.

It was immediately apparent that we had been casting flies too large, so we switched to Clouser Minnows dressed on regular size 4 hooks and cast them on 8-weight rods. Chartreuse and white was the ticket. But the first three strikes resulted in the morocoto crushing the bend of the hooks against the shanks in their powerful jaws.

During a few hours we managed to catch a number of them—the largest 22 pounds—and I have rarely had a fish that fought so hard. I was concerned that our rods might break. The guide said they get to about 40 pounds. I am not sure if you could land one that size on a fly outfit because small hooks are required.

# Pacific Sailfish     34

*Istiophorus platypterus*,
sail, spindlebeack, bayonetfish

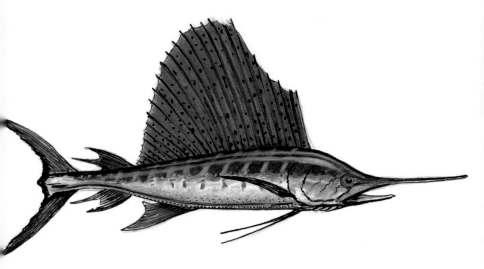

One of the most exciting fishing trips I made anywhere was in extreme northwestern Costa Rica during I think the late 1970s. It was here that I caught my first Pacific sailfish and several other ocean species that were new to me. I am 87 at this writing and am forgetting some names, but our captain's first name was Jim and I think his last name was Paddock. He was famous for chartering all over Central and South American offshore waters. His boat was about 40 feet and well laid out. My companion and I enjoyed the ride from the remote dock to just below the Nicaraguan border.

We arrived at our destination near dark and anchored in a long bay just off the Pacific Ocean. Jim carried us in a small skiff to a towering rock cliff, which we climbed to perhaps 50 feet above the bay. Here he dropped a bucket

on a long rope to a freshwater well he said had been dug by Spaniards explor-
ing the area centuries ago. I have always wondered how those explorers knew
where and how to dig that well—much of it through rock.

Costa Rica is one of the friendliest countries with the most wonderful
people of all the Central and South American countries I have visited and
fished. But we were anchored very close to the border of Nicaragua where
revolutionaries called Contras were battling the government for control.

The nights were pleasant with a light sea breeze, so Jim and his wife slept
above on the flying bridge while we were comfortable on air mattresses on the
open deck. Sometime after midnight, Jim quietly called to us to wake up. We
immediately rose, and in the dark stillness we could hear a soft, throbbing
thump, thump, thump, obviously of a motor. Jim instructed us to pick up the
two 8-foot killer gaffs, both armed with a large, sharp hook and a long, stout
shaft.

As the sound became louder, Jim turned on a huge searchlight that illumi-
nated the source of the sound. At the same time, he jacked a shell into his
shotgun—an unmistakable sound. Perhaps 200 yards away was a long
wooden boat with about ten men standing on the sides ready to board us.
Obviously they were Contra bandits.

As the brilliant light struck them, their boat engine went into high reverse,
backing away. Fluent in Spanish, Jim yelled something to them, and they
quickly left. It was obvious they were going to board and probably kill us and
steal the boat. Our captain was wise in the ways of local people and he no
doubt saved us from a disaster.

Even though I had the thrill of catching a huge sailfish as well as roosterfish and a variety of other species I had never before landed, that night in that
bay near Nicaragua was far more memorable than catching my first Pacific
sailfish on a fly.

# Hickory Shad 35

*Alosa mediocris,*
jumping jack

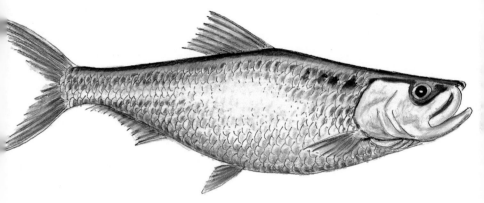

I n about 1949 I caught one of my first saltwater fish on a fly rod, and it was in fresh water. Tom McNally, outdoor editor for the *Baltimore Sun* papers, invited me to fish for hickory shad in Deer Creek just a few miles up from the head of the Chesapeake Bay. Tom said the hickories swarm into Deer Creek when local dogwood and shad bush bloom.

Using 4-weight rods and floating lines, we drifted tiny bright-colored flies through the schools of hickories filling this narrow stream. It was like rolling a wine bottle into a jail cell—there were so many hookups it was hard to count. Hickories rarely grow larger than a pound and a half, and they leap from the water like baby tarpon. We called them jumping jacks.

For many seasons after that, I made an annual pilgrimage to Deer Creek to catch hickories. Sadly, and for many reasons, the runs declined so badly that I finally stopped going—but I missed those spring trips for those jumping little fish on a light rod.

Two years ago Chuck Laughridge began to e-mail me photos of the fun he was having with hickory shad in his favorite river, the Roanoke, just below the Virginia border at Roanoke Rapids, North Carolina.

Chuck is as much fun to be with as anyone I have ever shared a boat with, and I hinted that maybe he would invite me and one of my best friends, Mark Lamos. Chuck did, and I am eternally grateful.

The Roanoke River is fairly large, averaging where we fished maybe 100 or more yards wide with deep pools. In the town of Roanoke Rapids, we had to wait our turn at the fine ramp to put in our boat just below the rapids for which the town is named.

Chuck's boat was perfect for us. Both he and Mark would not be considered small men, and his wide and stable boat made a perfect casting platform. Chuck knows this river as well as his home and anchored us only a few hundred yards from the ramp, while most other fishermen tore off downstream. At this location and one or two above the rapids, we frequently caught doubles—I had not caught so many hickories in decades. The Roanoke River is still unpolluted and offers not only quality hickory shad but striped bass fishing found in few freshwater rivers on the East Coast of the United States.

There were two extra pluses for me on this trip. One was the restaurant that offered Southern cooking, which I am very fond of. But most enjoyable was Chuck, who tells so many great stories and jokes and has the fastest comeback lip of anyone I have ever fished with.

# Sea-Run
# Brown Trout

# 36

*Salmo trutta*

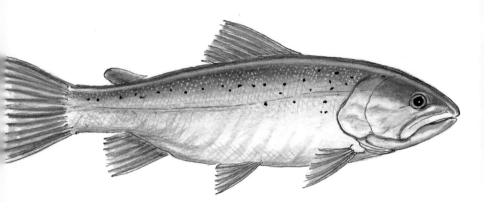

I've been fortunate to catch brown trout in the Traun River in Austria, some in Germany, in Chile, over much of the United States, and as far away as New Zealand, where I caught my largest brown—estimated by the guides to be 10 pounds.

For several years I was employed part-time by the terrific travel agency Frontiers International to take fly-fishing groups to remote parts of the world. One of these trips was to Kau Tapen Lodge in Tierra del Fuego, Argentina, located on the Rio Grande River at the extreme southern end of the country.

It is one of the most unusual places on earth. Stark is the word that comes to mind. It is rolling country of mostly grasslands, and sheep are the only farm animals I think can survive because of the hostile winters. Nowhere I have fished are there such strong winds. Because of the strong winds, there are almost no trees and the few that are there have all their limbs on the down-wind side of the trunk.

When Captain Cook arrived on his incredible exploratory trip, he found the native Indians clothed in furs and maintaining near-constant fires to keep themselves warm. Because they kept so many warming fires, he named the area Tierra del Fuego (Land of Fire).

**71**

The reason fly fishermen travel so far to fish there is the migratory run of huge sea-run brown trout that come out of the ocean and move up the Rio Grande. You have to want to fish here, for it requires an extended flight from the United States to Argentina, then another long flight to a tiny airport a few hours north, and then a car drive to Kau Tapen, a superbly managed fishing lodge of world class.

Our trip was before two-handed rods became popular in the states, and if I ever went back, I would certainly fish with them because of the wind. I caught several large brown trout, all as silvery as a steelhead. My best fish was estimated by the guide to be about 20 pounds, and it fought like one half again as big.

But what was memorable for me was the wind. I had never encountered anywhere a wind that was considered light at 25 mph. But I was grateful because I taught myself how to better cope with wind, and it gave me a casting edge when I faced a stiff breeze in other parts of the world.

# Cobia

**37**

*Rachycentron canadum,*
lemonfish, ling, crab eater

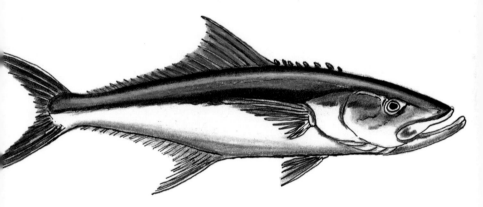

The cobia is a wonderful fly-rod fish and so resembles a shark when swimming that many mistake it for one. Cobia are shaped like a shark; the upper body is brownish in color, but the lower portion is rather white. But that's where the similarities end. Cobia are good eating, and years ago, when talking to an old-timer in Key West, I asked him what his favorite fish to eat was. Without hesitation he said, "Cobia."

Cobia have stiff pectoral fins that aid them when restricting the angler once hooked. When you try to land them, you find that they are incredibly strong, and any experienced angler will tell you never to put one in the boat that is green, or not tired.

I recall a famous light-tackle angler and friend who took me to the Dry Tortugas many miles west of Key West. We had chummed up a lot of cobia around a wreck and had caught several that weighed between 30 and 40 pounds. But one huge fish well over 60 pounds simply ignored our flies as it slowly swam around the boat time and again. My friend was really strong, and he asked me to open his huge fish box where he often kept some of his catch. "I am going to free-gaff that cobia when he comes around the next time," he said.

I gathered all my rods and reels and fled to the other end of his 28-foot boat. Watching with apprehension, I saw him snag the big cobia, lift it out of the water while it was thrashing violently, and try to drop it into the ample fish box. Instead, it fell on the deck where it went wild, thrashing around. It destroyed more than half a dozen of his rods and reels before my friend could club it unconscious.

My most memorable moment with cobia came not from catching one, but almost catching one. Rod Harrison and I were in a small boat cruising slowly along remote Melville Island when we saw a monstrous manta ray. The ray was a full 10 feet across and must have weighed more than a ton. Accompanying the ray were three cobia, one so huge I almost couldn't believe it. It may have been the largest I ever saw, possibly weighing 100 pounds or more.

Rod slowly eased the boat into position, and I tied on the largest Deceiver fly in my kit. I made a cast just in front of the huge cobia, and it flicked its tail, speeding up to intercept it, when from behind the monster a 40-pounder launched itself forward and grabbed the fly. I was so frustrated I never set the hook. It was the first time I did not want to catch a 40-pound cobia, and I often think what a thrill it would have been to hook and land that monster.

# Blue Trevally

# 38

*Carangoides ferdau*,
banded trevally, barred trevally,
Ferdau's trevally, Forskaal's jackfish

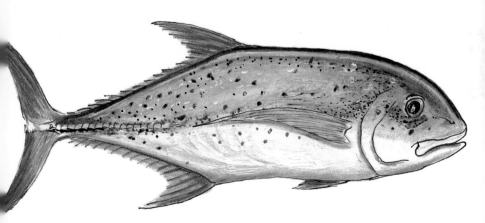

I was fortunate to take one of the early fly-fishing groups to Christmas Island, the largest atoll on earth, located 1,200 miles south of Hawaii in the vast Pacific Ocean, where I caught the giant trevally. The atoll is so-named because Captain Cook, the great English explorer, discovered the atoll on Christmas Day.

Among the first fly-fishing groups to arrive, we were taken in pairs by small pickup vehicles around the island and dropped off with a native guide. The drill was to wade the almost endless flats that teemed with bonefish.

Any experienced fly fisherman could catch 20 or 30 fish per day, there were so many bones. After several days of doing this I had caught so many bonefish I wanted to try something else. In those days we were transported to and from interior flats on a flat-bottom boat that leaked so badly that I told someone it was like being transported in a leaky fish live well.

When Captain Cook discovered Christmas Island he found there was a narrow opening in the atoll that allowed the tide to flow in and out. After several days of catching numerous bones, we were near this opening and I asked our guide if he would take me to the beach in the middle of the opening and come back for me in a few hours. Stepping out on the beach, I noted that for maybe 50 yards you could wade from shore on firm sand. With a box of mixed flies, I began slowly walking near the shore and almost immediately saw numerous fish. Casting smaller flies, I landed several sweet lips snapper (at least that was the name the guide gave me) and perhaps half a dozen fish in the 2- to 6-pound size that I never did identify.

I decided to wade deeper for a possible chance of catching larger species. In water just above my belt I saw a school of fish tearing into bait and worked close. I tossed a Deceiver into the mass and was immediately into a fish that was straining my 8-weight. Backing up until I was on the beach, I finally landed a beautiful fish I learned later was a blue trevally.

There are numerous species of trevallys in the Pacific Ocean, including the huge giant trevally that can exceed 100 pounds. The blue trevally flopping on the beach was about 20 pounds and shaped much like the jack crevalle we catch in Florida and the Bahamas—but much prettier. The back was blue-green with silvery sides and a few golden spots, and the fins were an iridescent blue, hence the name.

That fish had put up a great fight, and when I released it, it still seemed full of battle. The school was still out there, tearing into the bait, and during the next hour I landed perhaps eight or ten of these fish.

I recall many fine memories of the fantastic bonefish on my first trip to Christmas Island, but most of all I remember those blue trevally and how I was concerned with each one I hooked whether the 8-weight rod was up to the job.

# Striped Bass

**39**

*Morone saxatilis,*
striper, lineside, rockfish, rock

I started my saltwater fly-fishing career by first catching striped bass on the Chesapeake, casting popping bugs and small streamers. It was there in the late 1950s fishing for stripers that I first came up with the idea of making a fly that would not foul in flight, could be tied small or large, would be bait-shaped, and was easy to cast—thus was born the Lefty's Deceiver.

Since then I have caught striped bass with my great friend Dan Blanton on the West Coast in California as well as from Maine to South Carolina along the East Coast and in a number of freshwater lakes around the country. But I never could seem to land one larger than 30 pounds, although some came close.

My luck changed a few years ago. The Chesapeake Bay is where most of the East Coast stripers spawn. They overwinter in the bay's depths, and usually in April many of them move to the extreme upper end of the Chesapeake to gather in the shallows before going into the local rivers to complete their spawning.

The Chesapeake Bay is the sunken river mouth of the Susquehanna River, and there is a gathering area where the flowing freshwater part of the river meets the upper end of the bay. It's called the Susquehanna Flats. For several weeks, usually in April or early May, the flats hold big cow bass waiting for conditions to be just right before moving into the spawning rivers.

Since most of the flats are shallow, it is an opportunity for fly fishermen to catch really big fish—some have been caught (they must be released) nearing 50 pounds. It was on a calm early morning that I finally hit the mother lode of stripers.

My two friends and I were casting fairly large flies on 10-weight rods. My favorite fly is what I call a Magnum Deceiver—about 10 inches long but designed to cast like one much smaller and easier. We caught a number of fish between 14 and just under 25 pounds. Then the fishing gods smiled on me and I hooked and landed one that my friend said pulled his Boca Grip scale down to 37 pounds. I am now 87 years old, and I doubt if I will ever catch a bigger striper, but I have great memories of that huge cow bass when I released her and watched her disappear.

# Barramundi

# 40

*Lates calcarifer,*
giant perech, palmer, barra

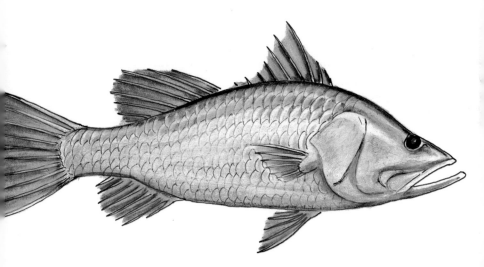

For many light-tackle anglers in Australia, the most popular and desirable fish to catch is the barramundi. I think it is in the same family as the snook. It has the same silvery color and sloping head as a snook and a sharp cutter on the gills—and most important, it tastes like a snook when cooked.

Today many impoundments in Australia have barramundi that grow to huge weights, topping even 50 pounds. But in the wild few barras are caught that large.

Rod Harrison and I were guests at the remote Bathurst Island Fishing Lodge in the late 1980s. The huge island is located off the northeast coast of Australia.

Few people fished there in those days, and I suspect not many do even today. All of the rivers on the island are affected by the tides. Rod and I had been fishing various spots along one river for barras when we came to a sharp bend. The water was surging against the curved bank, and it had eroded the bank so that a huge tree had fallen into the water. The river rushed at the tree and was deflected by the many limbs.

Wise in the ways of barramundi, Rod said, "Are we lucky! Lefty, there should be barras holding in among these sunken branches, catching bait coming downriver with the tide."

Anchoring the boat off to the side of the fast flow, we began to cast. For maybe 40 minutes almost every cast meant a hooked barra. These were not huge, maybe 6 to 12 pounds, but the number of barras holding there was astounding.

I have certainly caught bigger barras, but I never had as much fun as that day Rod and I threw our flies into what had to be a barramundi congregation.

# Guapote

# 41

*Parachromis* sp.

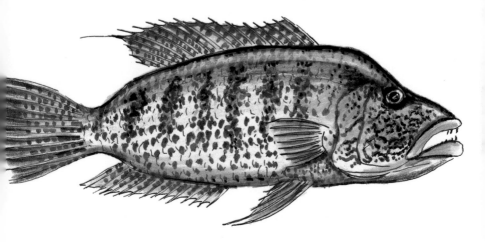

G uapotes are jungle fish inhabiting the fresh waters of eastern Costa Rica and Nicaragua. Though usually caught in the 2- to 5-pound size—rarely it gets to 12 to 15 pounds—it can hardly be matched for how hard it fights when hooked when you compare its size and strength with other freshwater species anywhere.

It is built for strength. The body is shaped somewhat like a permit but slightly more oval. It has long fins along most of the top and bottom of the body that extend to the large rounded tail. Grasp one and the body is unyielding—just hard muscle. In spawning season the males get a large lump on the forehead.

For a number of years in the 1960s through the 1980s I made trips to Casa Mar, a famous tarpon lodge located in extreme northeastern Costa Rica. The nearby Rio Colorado River was filled with 50- to 100-pound tarpon. On my second trip, after catching a number of these big fish, my guide suggested the next day to go for guapote. I had never heard of the fish and am always looking for a new species to test flies on.

The next morning the guide suggested I use an 8-weight rod and floating line and said he had a box of flies we would need. Getting in our 16-foot flat-bottom boat, we roared up the Rio Colorado and entered a narrow, winding jungle waterway named Monkey Creek. The young guide was showing off by rushing up the twisting narrow stream for more than a mile, the boat skidding around curves and causing me to duck overhanging vines and branches.

Slowing the boat to a crawl, we entered a jungle lagoon. Howler monkeys, supposed to have the loudest voice of any animal, protested our intrusion. The lagoon was walled in by giant trees, many covered with flowing vines with gorgeous flowers. One exceptionally large tree held many unusual nests resembling long stockings. The nests were constructed by the beautiful ora pendula birds, whose bodies were crow-black with long golden-colored tails. I was enthralled at the sight. The lagoon was about a half-mile long and quarter-mile wide, bordered on all sides by a profusion of lily pads.

Eduardo, my guide, suggested I use a tapered leader with a tippet of 20 pounds. I arched my eyebrows when he said 20 pounds. Doing as he suggested, I tied on a largemouth bass popping bug and cast to some nearby lily pads. I retrieved the bug maybe 10 feet, and there was a serious surface strike and the bug disappeared. Before I could react, the fish was in the lily pads, and when we reached the area, the tippet had broken. It was my first experience with a fairly large guapote.

I soon learned that the moment the bug disappeared you were in a street fight and you better apply immediate pressure. I was amazed at the size of the first guapote I caught. It weighed maybe 6 pounds, but I would have guessed 10 or 12.

The males with the large lump on their heads were the most aggressive. My biggest guapote we took back to camp since Eduardo wanted to eat it, so I was able to weigh it. It topped the scales at 10 pounds. I spent one more day catching guapotes on that tarpon trip and just had a ball.

Several years later I returned to that lagoon but never caught any guapotes larger than big bluegills. The aggressive large ones had been caught by other fly rodders visiting the camp. But I will always remember that a 10-pound guapote is all the freshwater fish I want to handle on a fly rod.

# Chain Pickerel 42

*Esox niger,*
jackfish, hammer handle, pickerel

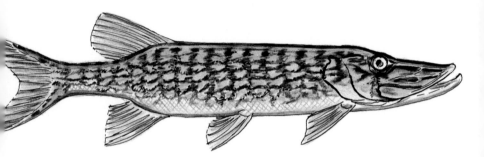

I live on the Western Shore of Maryland's side of the Chesapeake Bay. In the 1950s, the Eastern Shore was lightly populated—this was before they constructed the Bay Bridge at Annapolis, allowing easy access to the midportion of the shore—and to some degree it still is lightly populated.  In the spring when yellow perch spawn in the numerous streams on the Eastern Shore, several of us made the long trips from our homes in Frederick, which is in central Maryland, to catch them.

At this time of year the waters are chilly, and few fish are active other than perch and chain pickerel. The latter resemble miniature pike and rarely reach 4 pounds. Cool waters mean nothing to them, and they are great targets on a 4-weight trout rod. One of the best fly patterns is a 2½-inch red and white hackle streamer with a tiny bit of Mylar flash dressed on a 3X long hook. The 4-weight rod will easily cast this fly to 40 feet—all necessary to introduce it to a pickerel.

Small dams often stopped the yellow perch spawning runs, and it was just below them where the perch concentrated that we spent most of our time fly fishing. These dams were created to supply water to grind wheat and corn and were constructed in the earliest history of the country—many in the 1700s.

We always brought canoes with us when we fished the Eastern Shore, and once we had caught enough perch, we would use the canoe to paddle around the ponds above the dams. It was here that the pickerel would lie waiting to ambush our flies. A 2-pound pickerel on a 4-weight rod is a lot of fun.

In my canoe was one of my favorite fishing companions, Flip Kennedy, who was an excellent fly caster. There was a slight breeze blowing, and through no fault of Flip's, one of his forward casts was off target and buried the fly in my forearm. We had no idea where to find a doctor, and when I tried to pull it out with my hemostats I realized how much meat a hook barb holds.

Several weeks earlier I had attended an outdoor writers' conference where there was a demonstration on how to remove a hook by inserting a line under the bend, pressing down on the hook eye, and then giving a quick yank, removing the hook painlessly.

I explained the procedure to Flip, and with some trepidation got the line under the bend and held the hook eye against my arm. Holding my breath and nodding I was ready, Flip counted to three and yanked with the line and the hook miraculously leaped free.

Since then I have removed numerous hooks from people's flesh, although if it is near a tendon I take them to a doctor. I tell them I am going to yank the hook out at the count of three. I have found it works better if I count slowly and yank on the count of two instead of three.

You would not consider chain pickerel a great game fish, but when I think of them I recall trying for the first time that easy method of hook removal.

# Atlantic Sailfish 43

*Istiophorus albicans,*
spindlebeak

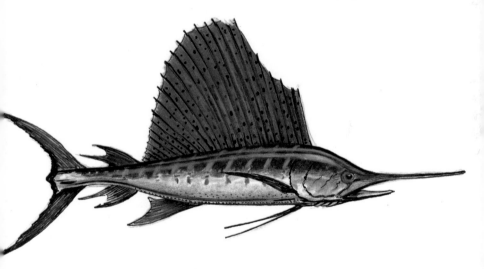

In 1964 famed outdoor writer Joe Brooks helped me get a job as manager of the Miami, Florida, MET Tournament—at the time the largest fishing tournament in the world. Leaving Maryland on the drive to the job, my son Larry, who began fishing at the age of four, was really excited about catching so many new fish in Florida.

My office was in the *Miami Herald* newspaper building, and Vic Dunaway was the paper's popular outdoor editor. We became instant friends, and I regard Vic as one of the best I have been so lucky to know. Within a week or so after I began my job managing the MET Tournament, Vic invited Larry and me to join him and his son Danny for a try at Atlantic sailfish. Larry slept little the night before; he was so excited.

We put in Vic's boat on upper Key Largo, and Vic soon motored to the edge of the Gulf Stream. He put out the blue runner baits and handed Larry the rod. While it was dead calm there were huge rolling swells that lifted the boat up and down. Before long I felt giddy and then downright seasick—and I had fished salt water in Maryland and other rough seas and had never experienced seasickness.

I felt so bad that I had to lie down in the boat. Not long after, I heard Vic, Danny, and Larry shouting. With an effort I raised up far enough to see Larry battling a jumping sailfish. Because of Vic's directions, he soon landed a beautiful sailfish. I had rarely seen Larry so excited.

When we quit for the day Vic brought the sailfish with us. Vic knew Al Pflueger, who owned Pflueger Taxidermy, the largest fish-mounting business in the world at that time. Al agreed to mount the sailfish for nothing, and it hung on our living room wall for many years.

When I think of the Atlantic sailfish, I have two thoughts: that Larry had caught his first, and while I fished many oceans thereafter and was only seasick several times in my career, I will never forget that new-to-me feeling that maybe I wanted to die.

# American Shad **44**

*Alosa sapidissima,*
shad

Back in the 1950s, each year Maryland witnessed two different shad runs in the Susquehanna River. The shad came in from the Atlantic Ocean, moved more than 100 miles up the bay, and entered the Susquehanna before their upstream progress was blocked by the huge Conowingo Dam. The smaller hickory shad then spawned in two creeks below the dam that fed the river. When the dogwood trees bloomed, these creeks teemed with hickories. A few weeks later, the much larger American shad, sometimes topping 7 pounds, would move up the Susquehanna River more than a mile until their progress was stopped by the dam.

Living in Frederick, Maryland, about 80 miles away, we knew about the American shad run and how treacherous the river below the dam can be. If little water is flowing through the dam, most of the rock-filled river below the dam is dry. When operators at the dam open turbine gates to release water, sirens warn people; some have ignored the sirens and paid the penalty. Negotiating the river when it is filled with water is difficult because of swift currents and the many hidden rocks.

I and three fishing friends of mine—Pete Demchak, Irv Swope, and Kit Nelson—decided we were going to catch shad below the dam. Putting in our canoes during high water, we struggled to paddle against the current to get near the dam where the shad concentrated.

Anchoring behind large boulders in the river, we had a fine time catching numerous big shad that jumped like baby tarpon when hooked. Several hours later, we were complimenting ourselves on how smart we were when we neglected to notice that the water seemed to be falling.

Not too long after that, we realized we had to get out of there. We upped the anchors and began frantically paddling downriver. Halfway to where we put in the canoes, the riverbed went dry as the operators shut down the turbine gates. We were stranded in what looked like a rock-filled graveyard. Having no choice, we got out of the canoes, intending on dragging them to the landing.

It was only then we realized how foolish we had been to stay too long. The bottom of the Susquehanna River was nothing but limestone rock covered in dark green slime. It was like trying to walk on greased bowling balls. The only way we could make it was to cling to our canoes and ever so slowly drag them along.

Had we quit an hour earlier, the return trip would have taken maybe 15 minutes. Instead, it was a horrible two hours. By the time we arrived at the landing, we had fallen so often that we were full of bruises and our clothes were covered in unpleasant slime.

I have since caught American shad in rivers from North Carolina to New England—but when I think of this species I always remember that downriver trip on the Susquehanna.

# Whitefish

45

*Prosopium williamsoni,*
whitey, Rocky Mountain whitefish

S cott Lake is a paradise if you enjoy fly fishing for northern pike and lake trout. It's located in northern Saskatchewan and can be reached only by floatplane. Some years ago Ken Gangler built several cottages and a lodge on a bluff overlooking miles of the huge lake dotted here and there with islands. Ken invited me to come fish Scott Lake.

It was a long trip that comprised landing at Chicago, followed by an overnight in Winnipeg and an extended flight in a small plane to a village on a river some distance from the lake. Finally a Beaver floatplane took me to the Scott Lake Lodge two days after I left home.

The fishing was worth the long trip, and I caught many big northern pike and lots of lake trout. Some of the best lake trout action required a long boat ride often across open and wind-lashed, boat-jarring water to a small river entering the main lake. Anchoring just off the mouth of the river and using Teeny 300-grain sinking lines and streamer flies, we had a wonderful time catching lake trout that averaged from 5 to 10 pounds.

I asked our guide what was up the river, and he said sometimes some really big pike, and so we went searching. We saw few pike but did find schools of fish weighing about 3 pounds apiece. The guide said they were whitefish and that people had tried but no one had been able to catch them. We tried various streamers with no luck and returned to the lodge.

Two days later the wind was calm and the lake like glass. Realizing it would be a long but comfortable boat ride, I went with the guide and a companion from California who also wanted to figure out how to catch these whitefish. We took a large assortment of flies to offer them.

The water in the stream was air-clear, and we could see schools of whitefish holding in the gentle flow. We cast popping bugs, all sorts of streamers, and a fly that seemed to work everywhere—the Woolly Bugger—without luck. They simply ignored our offerings.

The anchored boat was near the school, and I kept looking at the school of fish while eating lunch. Just before we finished eating, a good hatch of caddisflies emerged, filling the air around us. A lightbulb went on in my brain. I tied on a Gold-Ribbed Hare's nymph and allowed it to sink near the school. Several whitefish approached and turned away.

The water was incredibly clear, so I added 2 feet of thin 5X tippet to the fly, and on the first cast a whitefish took the nymph. We both rigged similar leaders and flies, and for the next hour until we spooked the fish, we had a great time. That was probably in the 1980s, and since then when fishing these distant northern lakes, I carry nymphs and a trout leader, and when I find whitefish I have a wonderful time with a light 5-weight rod.

# Dolly Varden

# 46

*Salvelinus malma,*
Dolly

Nope, this is not a lady but one of my favorite fish that swims in most of the lakes and streams in Alaska. It has some of the coloration of a brook trout but lacks the "worm marks" typical of a brook trout's back.

Two experiences stand out when I think about Dolly Varden, which many call Dollies.

Mead Johnson owned Mead Johnson Pharmaceutical Company (he told me he sold it for 200 million dollars) and asked me to help him learn to fly-fish. Perhaps a year later, in 1966, he said let's go to Alaska and you pick a place. Wow! I got right on it, but the trouble was in 1966 there really weren't many fishing lodges in Alaska. I finally settled on Yes Bay Lodge, which I think is still in operation near Ketchikan. Mead sent me a first-class ticket on what was then Northwest Orient Airline—now part of Delta.

Mead was from South Florida but was visiting California when I returned from a photo assignment in Bermuda. I checked only to find the airline was on strike. Hastily I tried to book another airline. In those days, few flights went to Alaska, and I could not get a booking.

Desperate, I called Mead's secretary and explained the problem. Her answer was, "Mr. Johnson is going to be very disappointed." I thought to myself, not nearly as much as me, who might miss a trip to virgin Alaska—and he was paying me $350 a day, which also meant a disappointment for my wife, who handled our bills.

In the end Mead chartered a Learjet that picked me up at a private airport near my home. I flew with a pilot, copilot, and a steward directly to Ketchikan. Ten hours after leaving my home near Miami, I met Meade as I stepped off the plane.

Fishing there was unlike anything I ever witnessed in fresh water. Mead engaged a bush pilot who stayed with us every day. He would fly us to some remote place and we would catch fish. Mead may have been the most impatient man I ever knew and after half an hour or so we loaded up and would fly to another location.

One day while flying over the wilderness I looked down and saw a lake shaped somewhat like a banana. I asked the pilot if there was any fish there. He told me he never saw anyone fish it—so we landed.

We taxied down the lake to where a stream entered and immediately began hooking rainbows and Dolly Varden. Dollies are excellent eating, so we kept a few for our shore lunch. After lunch the guide walked back a hundred yards to an ancient log cabin. We heard him yelling; thinking he might have met a bear, we grabbed the shotguns and ran toward him. Running out of the bush he held a small, green, silk purse. Upon opening it he had found maybe a dozen silver dollars, all black as coal and dating back to the early 1900s. Apparently some trapper had lived there and this was his little cache of money. He died and for more than 50 years that silk purse had lain in the rafters of the old cabin.

The guide took the blackened dollars back to camp and used silver polish to restore them, but I would have left a few in the condition he first found them.

# Bluegill

# 47

*Lepomis macrochirus*,
bream, copperhead

Today Capt. Sarah Gardner is a legendary captain from the Outer Banks of North Carolina who has helped her clients catch world-record fish and has some world records of her own. Sarah was like a daughter to my wife and me, and years before she became a captain, we were wading a small stream in central Maryland. The region used to be dotted with such small streams that laced through farmlands. Because of overdevelopment in the area, the huge number of homes have depleted the groundwater table, so today those streams are only a trickle. Our goal was catching bluegills and smallmouth bass on fly and ultralight spinning tackle.

The drill was to park the car by a stream that rarely exceeded 40 feet in width. Donning old tennis shoes, we carried only a rigged fly rod and a spinning rod and a small box holding a few flies and lures. We waded always upstream and cast into the many pockets of water, some only a foot deep. If we waded downstream, the roiled water stirred by our feet alerted the fish and we would catch less.

This is one of the most relaxing and fun-filled ways you can fish on a warm summer day, and the aggressive bluegills didn't hesitate to grab our offerings that invaded their domain. Now and then you could land a small-mouth bass, but rarely one more than 2½ pounds.

On this day I had a magazine assignment about catching bluegills on fly and ultralight tackle in small creeks. I asked Sarah to join me, and I am here to say I have never known anyone who enjoys fishing more than Sarah.

Parking the car near one of my favorite bluegill streams, Sarah grabbed a rod. I carried the other one and my camera gear. We began wading, and she soon caught several bluegills.

I had fished this stream with the landowner's permission for years with one of my oldest friends, Paul Crum. What I did not know was that someone from the city had bought the land. It is my observation that when people from the city buy land in the country, the first thing they do is put up no-trespassing signs, alienating local people. When we parked the car, I saw some new no-trespassing signs but assumed the landowner whom I had known for years would not mind if we fished there.

Sarah and I were enjoying the moment. She was catching bluegills, and I was getting some photos I needed for the story. Fortunately we were still close to our parked car when we heard several dogs barking. We could see toward the old farmhouse and realized that three huge—and I mean huge—nasty dogs were running across the field in our direction. Sarah and I ran to the car, arriving well before the dogs.

I learned later that someone from Baltimore or Washington had moved to the area and purchased the farm—and of course put up no-trespassing signs, planning to enforce them with nasty dogs.

It wasn't until we got home that I realized I left one of my favorite ultra-light spinning rods and reels. Apparently in the rush to elude the dogs I had completely forgotten the outfit.

I have caught bluegills in many states, but maybe the most memorable incident for me was the headlong flight to the car Sarah and I made to elude those dogs.

# Yellowfin Tuna 48

*Thunnus albacares,*
Allison tuna

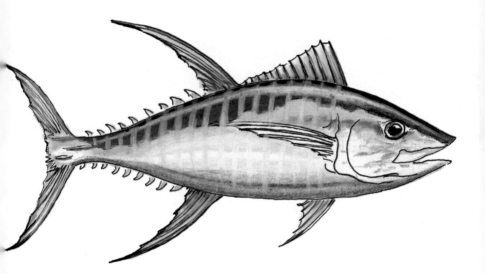

The yellowfin tuna is one of the toughest fish you can fight, especially if you are offshore, where they often reach weights exceeding 100 pounds. Tuna of any type are all muscle and have a sickle tail. Any experienced fly fisherman will tell you a fish with a sickle tail is going to give you trouble—no matter the species. Only once did I almost catch a yellowfin when not well offshore.

Rod Harrison, legendary fishing writer from Australia, had arranged a trip to the wild and remote New Britain Island, part of Papua New Guinea. From my home in Maryland it took 32 flying hours to get there.

My trip began in a giant 747 jet to Los Angles, a slightly smaller jet to Australia, and even smaller jet to Darwin. Then we flew to Port Moresby in a two-engine plane. From there we were transported in a one-engine plane to New Britain, landing on an old World War II dirt strip. We got in a pickup truck and drove down the mountain to the biggest log canoe I ever saw, maybe 60 feet long. It transported us to a tiny island lying maybe two miles offshore, which the Australians named Argem.

Greeting us were perhaps 40 native men and women with bones in their hair who carried bows and arrows. The women adorned themselves with gray scars they put on their bodies to be attractive to the men. At first I was intimidated, but all were very pleasant.

The person arranging the trip had the natives build three huts for our stay from local palm trees. (The natives seemed comfortable in the jungle behind the houses.) What was astounding was that whoever had built our thatched houses in this remote area had also constructed a separate flush toilet. During our entire stay, natives would go to the toilet and flush it and shake their heads as they saw the swirling water disappear in the bowl—to them this was some sort of magic.

But back to the yellowfin tuna. This part of New Guinea offers fabulous inshore and offshore fishing. One day just 200 yards from shore we saw a 7-foot marlin chasing 4-foot long dolphin, which were using their tails to escape by running upright on the surface. In the distance but clearly visible from the island were schools of tuna crashing the surface. Some of the schools were perhaps a half-mile long.

Our quarry was the Niugini black bass that lived in the freshwater rivers along the nearby shore. One day we returned for lunch, and after eating we were resting in the shade. The shoreline of our island was sandy and extended out maybe 20 feet before dropping off into deep water.

I was in a hammock and dropped off to sleep when I heard a lot of splashing. I looked and not 30 feet from shore were yellowfin tuna trapping large baitfish against the sand. I leaped up, grabbed my 12-weight rod armed with a large Deceiver fly, and rushed to the shore. Wading out, I tossed the fly into the thrashing tunas and was rewarded with an instant hookup.

Yards of fly line and backing disappeared from the reel in one of the fastest-escaping fish runs I've experienced. I would regain line and then lose it over and over. Things began to look better for me when I finally had much of the fly line on the reel and sensed the tuna was weakening. Then the tuna touched the sand and that lit a fire under it. It began such a strong run I realized I might lose my line and my backing. We had a minimal amount of tackle with us, so I lowered the rod, clamped on the spool, and broke the tippet.

Whenever I think about yellowfin tuna I remember the one I almost landed while standing hip deep off remote New Britain Island.

# Hog Snapper

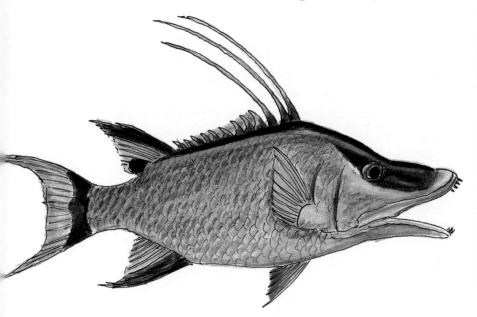

*Lachnolaimus maximus,*
hog fish, hog wrasse

Few would contest after eating one that the hog snapper is the best-tasting of all the snappers in tropical waters. The meat is pure white with virtually no veins and it is simply delicious.

In the early 1970s, Pete Perinchief, the head of the Bermuda Fishing Bureau, invited me to test their waters and write about it so others could enjoy it. Bermuda is a small island shaped like a fishhook on the eastern edge of the Gulf Stream.

It was a two-hour flight from New York, and when I walked down the plane's stairs, I saw a policeman at the base clad in the famed Bermuda shorts. Formerly a British colony, Bermuda and its inhabitants still maintain a little of the proper way the British feel things should be done. Immediately behind me coming down the stairs were three hippies with long hair dressed in shoddy clothing. The officer asked them to claim their luggage. After everyone had deplaned, he ordered them back on the plane with their luggage and said they would return to New York. That was my introduction to Bermuda.

Pete put me up in a classy place called Cambridge Beaches. To give you an idea of how nice, each morning someone on a bicycle arrived with a pre-ordered breakfast in a large tray held aloft with one hand.

I was to stay for a week and sample inshore and fabulous offshore waters. One evening Pete said he would be tied up until noon the next day and suggested wading on the clear sand flat nearby for bonefish, which he said would be tough to catch but large. He was right, and the first several bones I saw were spookier than a cat in a dog pound. I did finally catch one—it was a solid 8 pounds and I was elated.

By midmorning the tide had risen so that it was hip deep, but the fish were still fairly easy to see due to the water's clarity. At the edge of the flat was some coral rock, and I saw a fish definitely not a bone investigating the crevices. I cast a fly to it, got an immediate take, and the fight was on. The fish was strong but fought like a bulldog instead of making long runs. I was stunned when I finally landed it and wished for a camera but was alone. It was a hog snapper of about 8 pounds. I caught one more on another coral rock pile. Never since have I seen hog snappers on the flats.

# Royal Peacock Bass

# 50

*Cichla intermedia*,
peacock bass, pavon

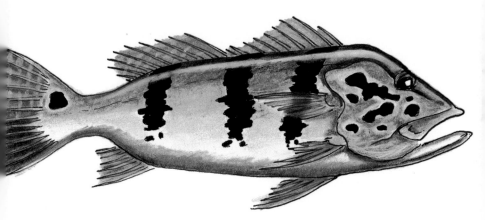

There are a number of species of the jungle fish peacock bass. Our Amazon native guide called the fish that my old fishing buddy Simon Goldseker caught a royal peacock bass. That's a day I won't forget.

Simon is a widely experienced fly rodder in both fresh and salt water, and we have enjoyed a number of exotic trips. We were fishing in the upper Amazon basin and living in pup tents. This was before the days of mother ships and modern bass boats, which you now see on these waters.

During the early part of the day, Simon and I had great fun with big peacock bass. Having been on other trips, I suggested to Simon we use underwater flies, and long Lefty Magnum Deceivers and Half and Half patterns, mostly in black and orange, worked well.

I had urged all on the trip to bring good rain gear. I remember taking a group of CEOs to the region and telling them it was in a rain forest and to bring rain gear. Two didn't.

After eating lunch in the boat, we noted that it was clouding over. Before too long it became almost dark and Simon, the guide, and I donned rain gear. The guide began cruising the shoreline, obviously looking for something. Finally he pulled into an area where there were trees overhanging the river lower than those nearby, very dense with leaves. It was the shelter he was looking for.

The heavens opened up and we sat hunched in thankfully good rain gear while it poured. At one time the raindrops were the size of marbles. I have a photo of Simon and the guide hunched over and getting splattered with those raindrops.

As quick as it came, it disappeared and fishing picked up. Simon caught a beautiful peacock, which the guide called a royal peacock bass. It was very different from the big three-barred peacocks we had been catching, which can exceed 20 pounds. This one was about 5 pounds, and the guide said they never got much bigger. When I think about those peacock bass, I always remember one of the most torrential rains ever.

# Blackfin Tuna

## 51

*Thunnus atlanticus*,
football, Bermuda tuna

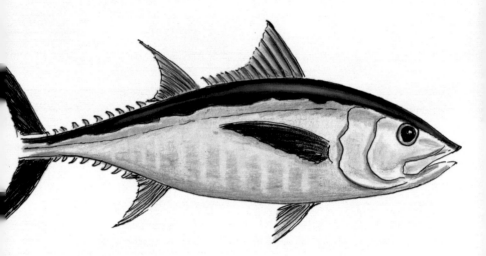

I have never been interested in claiming world records, although in the 1960s for monetary reasons I did claim twelve.

My first world record on a fly was a blackfin tuna. This is a beautiful fish. The belly is silvery with a yellowish line above, and the back is the most intense black I have ever seen on a creature. Freshly caught and lifted from the water, the black back almost glows. When one is fought on a 10-weight rod the fly fisherman has all he wants to handle. While blackfins can obtain weights in excess of 30 pounds, most that are caught on flies range from 15 to 22 pounds.

Lefty Regan from Key West was a true pioneer of offshore fly fishing and with Dr. Web Robinson developed the method of teasing fish to boatside and then substituting a fly for the teaser. In South Florida during the 1960s more records and tournament winners were caught on Lefty's Cay Sal boat than with any other captain.

In those days I managed the huge MET Tournament, which covered all of South Florida and the Keys. Lefty and I became fast friends and much of what I learned about offshore fly fishing I owe to him.

"How would you like to catch a blackfin tuna on a fly rod?" Lefty asked me. Naturally I jumped at the chance. Lefty, his mate Junior, and I left the Garrison Bight Key West docks and in less than 40 minutes we were cruising the edge of the Gulf Stream.

Not long after, Junior and Lefty both yelled, "Blackfins!" I could see tuna leaping upward out of the water as they slashed into a school of baitfish. Lefty raced to get well ahead of them. Two weeks before I had been given a Fin-Nor number three fly reel by Henry Breyer, the owner of the company. This would be the first test for it, and I was eager.

We pulled well ahead of the tuna, and Lefty slowed the boat, allowing me to cast directly in front of the oncoming blackfins. As the 6-inch white Deceiver fly fell to the surface, a blackfin rose from the water, leaping at least 4 feet in the air, and turned toward the fly. I am certain the tuna saw the fly while in midair, for it appeared to be twisting its tail and body, making adjustments as it dove toward the target and hit it!

This was in 1965, and I hadn't yet tangled with any kind of tuna. I set the hook and line began disappearing faster than I could imagine. The black handle was nothing more than a blur—but the reel drag was flawless.

Then the fight began. I would recover line and then lose it only to regain it, and this happened again and again. The reel was a direct drag, and when the escaping tuna would pull line from it, the handle would be ripped from my hand. I was unaware that before long my finger gripping the handle was a bloody mess.

After perhaps a ten-minute slugfest, mate Junior was able to lift the tired blackfin from the water. Back at the dock, it was weighed and witnessed and became my first world record: a 19-pound, 4-ounce blackfin. After a round of picture-taking Lefty was chuckling, and I asked him why. "What color is your shirt?" "It's white, why?" He answered: "It's now red and white." Looking down, I saw that the shirt was dotted with spots of blood from my mangled finger.

# Barracuda

# 52

*Sphyraena* sp.,
great barracuda, 'cuda

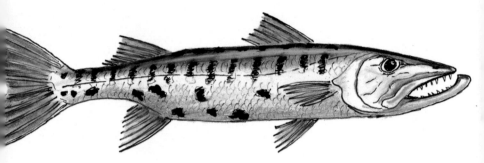

I have caught many barracudas with the fly, but one I did not catch is the most memorable. If you have not fished for 'cudas, you have no idea how swift they move on the strike. I once wrote in an article for *Florida Sportsman* magazine that "I have seen a barracuda before and after it struck but never while it was striking." One moment you are looking at a 'cuda poised to strike your fly and the next you are hooked up.

The memorable event occurred in the Dry Tortugas, where there is a fort made entirely of brick sitting on a tiny coral island surrounded by a protective rocky reef. In the 1960s when my teenage son Larry and I were there, the only fishermen were shrimpers who would drag their nets at night and then come into the harbor near the fort to cull their catch. They would select their shrimp and use snow shovels to push overboard all the unwanted small fish, crabs, and other creatures they accidentally caught in their nets. There were so many mutton snappers living the harbor that the water would turn pink as huge schools of them would rise to gorge on the creatures pushed overboard. It was a gigantic chum line, and all Larry and I needed to do was cast a small fly into the swirling mass of snappers and there would be a hookup.

The Dry Tortugas had been designated as a National Park, and the ranger in charge of Everglades National Park was also charged with overseeing the Dry Tortugas. I became good friends with him, and on three occasions he allowed Larry and me to fly to the Tortugas on one of their supply flights. The plane would land in the deep water next to the boat dock. We had to bring our own food and bedding, and we slept in one of the brick structures inside the fort.

The only caretaker was I think named Whitey Hopkinskill. He loved being there, and his hobby was collecting crabs and other hard-shelled creatures. After removing the insides, he would dry them. He had many crabs, lobsters, starfish, and other dried things. The most impressive one he collected from the moat surrounding the fort was the shell of a Florida spiny lobster many call a langouste. The shell, including the antennae, was almost 6 feet long. We had never seen one even half that size. After Whitey died, Larry and I often wondered what happened to the wonderful collection of dried creatures—and especially that Florida lobster.

But back to the barracuda. There was one other small island near the fort called Loggerhead. Not far to west of it in less than 20 feet of air-clear water lay the remains of an old, small ship. Since virtually no one fished there in those days, the waters around the shallow wreck were filled with fish. It was like a giant aquarium. Larry and I would often go there in Whitey's little skiff just to watch.

One day a school of cero mackerel rushed over the wreck, slashing into many of the smaller fish. I quickly threw a small Deceiver fly into the mackerel and was rewarded with a hard strike and a fast-escaping fish. The cero is perhaps the most beautiful of all mackerels, and at the time the world record on fly was maybe 10 pounds. This fish was easily 20 pounds and far larger than any I'd seen. Larry and I were excited. Finally we had the mackerel at boatside when out of nowhere a huge barracuda appeared. It started at the tail and engulfed the large mackerel to just behind the gills, and closing its jaws, it disappeared. I still have the photo of what was left of the head and body just behind the gills.

How big was that 'cuda? I have no idea, but I am willing to swear it was at least 6 feet long and maybe 100 pounds. In fishing around the world, I have seen many big 'cudas, but none that approached this one in size. Each day Larry and I would go back to the area hoping to see or hook it but all in vain.

# Bluefish

# 53

*Pomatomus saltatrix*,
blue, snapper blue, chopper

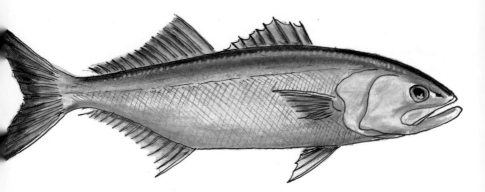

Most fly fishermen who fish the northern Atlantic inshore waters of the United States will agree that the hardest-fighting fish for its size is the bluefish. It is the most aggressive fish in these waters, and in a chum line I have actually seen them gorge themselves, regurgitate the chum, and continue to eat more. It is not unusual for one to bite another in a school.

They can be difficult to catch sometimes, especially when finning on a calm surface. But I like bluefish because you rarely meet one that isn't hungry, and they are not too choosy about fly patterns. In short, they are wonderful fly rod fish.

Bluefish are cyclic, and about every 40 years they are found in huge numbers and large sizes. During the 1970s along the Atlantic coast from New England to the Outer Banks of North Carolina there were tremendous numbers of bluefish, often from 12 to 16 pounds and a few even larger. It was a bonanza for fly fishermen. You could catch them in a chum line well offshore or even inshore from small boats where the hungry packs savaged local baitfish schools.

Don Peters and Paul Banker were two fishing friends of mine. Don had a wonderful bluefish spot in less than 6 feet of water close to the shoreline just below the Chesapeake Bay Bridge in Maryland. Don and I are avid fly fishermen while Paul preferred spinning tackle. Starting just after dawn more than 200 yards from shore, we began catching bluefish of 6 to 12 pounds. Don and I cast popping bugs while Paul preferred a ⅜-ounce Atom Popper plug.

For several hours we caught one blue after another, a few more than 12 pounds. Paul was a quiet man, but it was obvious he was enjoying himself. Moreover he was catching six fish to every one we boated on the fly.

As Paul released another 12-pounder, Don said, "Paul, you really ought to try fly casting; it's a lot of fun."

Paul said nothing but after he made another cast and had an immediate hookup I looked at the grin on his face and said to Don, "I don't think this is a good time to convince Paul to use fly tackle."

# Amberjack

# 54

*Seriola* spp.,
AJ, amberfish

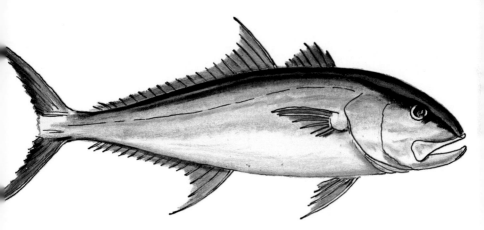

A favorite method of mine for testing fly rods that will be used offshore is to hook up with amberjack. Offshore rods require little long-distance casting, but they must have lifting power. Hooked fish try to escape by descending into the depths, and the only way to bring them to the boat is by using a rod that is strong enough to physically lift them.

A small amberjack is in the 20- to 30-pound class and some exceed 100 pounds. Few fish fight harder or longer. The best way to test a prototype rod is to place a piece of meat on the leader and lower it into an amberjack's dining room. It will soon be apparent if the rod will stand the torture of fighting and lifting offshore fish.

But that is not the purpose of this tale. Capt. Gainey Maxwell back in the 1960s was the first charter skipper in Key West to routinely run the 75 miles over open water to fish his clients in the fabled Dry Tortugas. I made that trip several times with him, and the fishing was incredible.

My job at the time was to manage the MET Tournament. People competed by entering the largest of each species; the even-more-coveted prize was to catch a fish that would be considered a MET record. Only tournament member Lee Cuddy and I were commissioned to validate a MET record.

The tournament covered all of South Florida. Sometimes the angler lived hours from the Miami tournament headquarters, and it took a day or two before Lee or I could weigh a possible MET record. All too often if we didn't weigh the fish until two or three days after a catch, the weight they claimed and the one we saw on our scales were not the same. Anglers complained that their fish lost weight between catch and our weighing, so they lost the possible record.

The last day I fished with Captain Maxwell in the Dry Tortugas, I used 150-pound offshore rod and reel to land a huge amberjack. I brought along a cotton scale, which is simply an iron bar with a sliding weight, and on it the fish weighted 102 pounds. We placed it in Gainey's fish box at the transom of the boat, and there was no ice. We closed the lid and headed back to Key West the next morning. About 24 hours later I again weighed the amberjack on the same cotton scale, and as I recall it lost only a pound or two.

Driving home, I thought about this. The next week I was called to Homestead, Florida, a short drive from the office, where I weighed a tarpon hanging in a cold-storage locker. I knew the owner of the fishing shop and asked him if I could leave the tarpon hanging several days and then come back and reweigh it. He agreed. When I returned, to my great surprise it had lost a lot of weight.

Over the next few months I weighed a number of fish for the tournament and came to this conclusion. If it was a grouper, snapper, tarpon, redfish, bonefish, or largemouth bass, it could lose a lot of weight. If it was a sailfish, cobia, brown trout, or shark, it would lose relatively little weight during a fairly short time.

The reason was the scale structure of the fish. Fish like tarpon have large scales, and if the body starts to dry out, the scales begin to lift, allowing even more body fluids to evaporate. But tight scales on fish like the cobia or freshwater trout tend to slow the evaporation process. It's best to keep the fish wet until it's weighed to prevent evaporation.

# Rainbow Runner

# 55

*Elagatis bipinnulata,*
rainbow jack, Spanish jack, runner

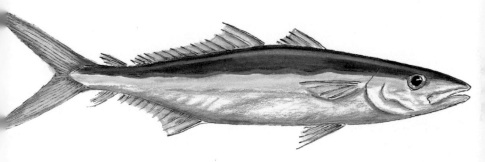

This is a beautiful fish I have sometimes compared to the male wood duck, one of the prettiest of all ducks. The rainbow runner lives in the open ocean, and once you see one, you will always recognize them. It has a white belly and dark olive back, but in between there are a number of strikingly bright colors ranging from light blue to yellow. It's a long, sleek fish and has the sickle tail of the jack family.

On some of my trips to Bermuda, we fished off Challenger Bank, a large sea mount rising out of the ocean depths about 7 miles offshore. We anchored on the edge and began chumming. The favorite chum is hogmouth fry, a tiny baitfish. Charter skippers carry a liberal supply, and fish show up even in this vast ocean once a chum line starts dropping a constant flow of tiny dead baitfish in the water.

You never know what will appear in the cobalt-blue waters behind the boat. It can be anything from billfish to small snappers. Casts are usually only made a few feet behind the boat, and it's some of the most exciting fly rodding anyone can imagine. If you ever get a chance to go to Bermuda in June or July and fish Challenger Bank, the memory will stay with you—I promise.

On one of these trips I brought along an 8-weight rod—light for this kind of fishing—with a freshwater reel that had no drag but had a rim control so I could apply hand pressure during a fish fight. While standing at the transom and watching the different fish streak through the chum line, I noticed some really beautiful fish and asked Pete Perinchief, head of Bermuda's fishing bureau, what they were. Pete looked and said excitedly, "Good Lord, those are huge rainbow runners."

They didn't look too big, so I thought I'd try to land one on my little 8-weight rod. I dropped a small white fly among them and allowed it to sink unimpeded to imitate the chum. Instantly I was hooked up, and the reel spun so fast that while I palmed the rim it actually got hot against my hand—something I had never felt before. The tippet was a 6-pound-test so drag pressure had to be gentle and luckily it was a relatively soft fiberglass rod.

I fought that fish for perhaps 15 minutes, and it made a number of long runs. Finally Pete netted it and brought it aboard. He was really excited. "I am sure this is a world record for rainbow runners," he declared. Pete wrapped the fish in a wet towel and stored it on ice for the trip home.

Back at the dock, it was weighed and Pete certified it as a member of the International Game Fish Committee. I am embarrassed now to say I don't remember the weight, but it was about 6 or 8 pounds. It held the record for the largest rainbow runner caught on 6-pound test tippet and was only surpassed when they eliminated the 6-pound class for the 8-pound class. It was certainly one of the prettiest fish I have caught.

# Largemouth Bass

# 56

*Micropterus salmoides,*
big mouth, bucketmouth, green bass, Florida bass

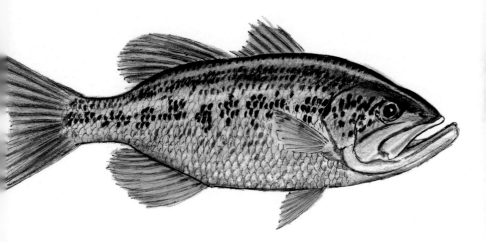

believe every state in the union excepting maybe Alaska has largemouths. I had fun in the 1950s catching them in Mexico and as far north as some of the provinces of Canada. I recall the first really big one I caught—it weighed 7 pounds, and in Maryland where I lived that was huge one. I decided to try something different and used popping bugs on dark nights in many of the local farm ponds. There was one pond a local farmer wouldn't allow anyone to fish, but I realized he'd never know if I fished after midnight. Sure enough I caught a dozen nice ones and that 7-pounder. I did put them all back.

In 1957 Tom Cofield, another outdoor writer friend, and I went to Florida to Lake Lochloosa. After some research, Tom said the locals fished with golden shiners, so we took along our minnow bucket we used at home. I think it held about a gallon and a half of water plus our minnows. We stayed at a fish camp that was so rustic that calling it a camp was being kind. There was a board-walk over a swampy area you had to walk on to reach the boat we rented. The first morning I heard the owner's dog barking at a rattlesnake on the ramp that was honest to God nearly 6 feet long. I alerted the owner, and he shot it with a .22 rifle. For years afterward I showed people the photo of him holding it aloft by the tail. Fortunately that was the only snake we had to have dispatched.

While I have caught largemouths in the Everglades canals when I lived near Miami that were up to 11 pounds, this first trip to Florida is what I remember when I think about largemouth bass. The first morning Tom and I were up at dawn, and as soon as we saw a light in the camp owner's shop we took our minnow bucket over to buy some golden shiners. The camp owner seemed amused. "What ya gonna put the shiners in?" he asked. I held the minnow bucket up. He then showed us the shiners we were to use. Each was at least 8 inches long. Our bucket could not have held two and kept them alive. Suffice it to say we bought the largest minnow bucket we had ever seen. Of course we needed larger hooks—and the floats we used were almost the size of tennis balls.

The old man knew what he was talking about, for we caught huge largemouth bass and their backs were shiny black. When I think of largemouth bass, I always remember that rattlesnake and the old man chuckling when I handed him our minnow bucket.

# Queenfish

## 57

*Scomberoides* sp.,
leatherskin, queenie, giant dart

I n 1987 Rod Harrison, Australia's senior fishing writer, arranged for me to
fly there for several weeks of fishing with him. We had a fantastic time.
One week we were flown by floatplane from the small town of Kununurra
in northern Australia to a remote outback river called the Drysdale. Our camp
was in a desert and our tents made from mosquito netting since they antici-
pated it wouldn't rain. It was possibly the most remote fishing area in all of
Australia. We never saw another person or heard a jet plane. Near us was a
huge colony of large flying-fox bats that filled the skies each night as they
spread out to feed.

The river shores were paved with saltwater crocodiles, which we carefully
avoided while catching a number of hard-fighting species. One day we fished
our way down to where the Drysdale River entered the Arafura Sea. We had
lunch on a sandy beach at the river's mouth. I have always been interested in
birdlife, and in a tree on the sand dune behind us were a pair of familiar-
looking birds. After lunch we took a nap and when I awoke I walked to the

tree, which was maybe 30 feet high. The birds perched there were peregrine falcons. They looked down at me when I stood under the tree. They seemed curious, and I am sure they had seen few humans and were completely unafraid. It was a special moment for me.

One of the best tricks to lure fish in salt water so the fly rodder can offer a fly to an excited fish is a chugger. This is a spinning or plug-casting surface lure with a cupped face and no hooks. The angler throws it out and immediately begins retrieving by snapping and jerking with the rod. This causes the chugger to make loud noises and splash the water—that really turns on many species. Once the fish appear and attack the chugger, the angler removes it from the water, and the fly fisherman drops his fly in its place. Almost always a strike follows.

After a lunch and pleasant nap, we got in the boat and anchored where the Drysdale River enters the sea. Rod threw the chugger out and began bringing it back with loud whooshing sounds. Immediately it was attacked, and I rifled a Deceiver fly that landed near the chugger. Two strips and I was hooked into a queenfish that immediately went airborne.

These are great fun on a fly rod. A large one is maybe 12 pounds, and we hooked a few near that size. Their bodies are rather long and flat and mostly silver in color, hence the name. The Australians often refer to them as "queenies." When hooked, they jump a lot, and if they turn that flat body sideways to the angler, the fight resembles one with a jack crevalle. They are often found in schools much like bluefish, so if you locate one, you're in for some fun. Rod and I spent a pleasant half hour hooking, landing, and releasing queenies. It was late afternoon when we made the fairly long run upriver to our camp. I'll always remember those falcons looking at me as if they didn't know a human and the fun Rod and I had with queenfish—it was special day.

# Lemon Shark 58

*Negaprion brevirostris*,
brown shark

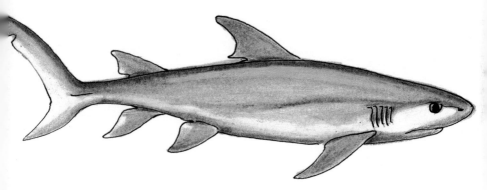

There are two popular sharks that fly rodders target on the flats in Florida and the Caribbean: the blacktip and the lemon. Of the two, I find the lemon shark to be more unpredictable and more aggressive. When poling the flats, the pole's foot often stirs the muddy bottom. Both blacktip and lemon sharks have grabbed the pole's foot, apparently thinking it was something to eat. When wading for bonefish, I've had blacktips approach—if they get too close, slapping the rod down on the water scares them away. But this is not so with all lemon sharks. On several occasions I have had to hit them on the nose with the butt of the rod as I made my way out of the water.

The scariest event with a lemon occurred off Key Largo when I hooked a nice bonefish of maybe 7 pounds. Just before I was able to lift it in the boat to release it, an excited lemon showed up. I quickly grabbed the bonefish, and as I lifted it from the water, the lemon rushed in, grabbed the tail, and tore the fish from my hands. Needless to say I was shook.

When I think of lemon sharks I also think of my son Larry. In 1964 I moved my family to Miami to manage the largest fishing tournament in the world at that time, the MET Tournament. Larry, age 13 and an avid outdoorsman, shot his first squirrel from a canoe while drifting a Maryland river when he was 6, and he had caught scads of local fish.

Of course he didn't know how to pole a boat, and I enjoyed poling him for all the new species such as boxfish, redfish, snook, and tarpon. We had memorable days together.

I got an assignment from *Field and Stream* magazine to do a story about fly rodding for sharks on the flats, which at the time few people were doing. There were lots of lemon sharks on the backside of Elliott Key in Biscayne Bay, so I motored quietly on the flat at high tide and sure enough a number of lemons were cruising the flat with their dorsal fins sticking out of the water.

I had Larry stand on the front of the boat holding my rod rigged with a shark fly. I began to pole after a shark. Unless you ever tried to pole after a shark, you never realize how fast they are moving. When I was within casting distance, I ran forward, handed Larry the boat pole, and grabbed the fly rod. By that time the shark was out of casting range. This happened four times. Finally I anchored the boat and said, "Larry, today you are going to learn to pole."

We spent the next two hours with Larry learning to pole. Surprisingly, Larry really enjoyed both learning it and being able to pole me to fish. The tide was gone and so were the sharks. But a few days later we got the fish and photos I needed for the magazine article, and I would not have been able to do it without him.

# Black Drum

## 59

*Pogonias cromis*,
drum, striped drum

S altwater black drum are not considered wonderful gamefish even though they can obtain great size. They feed mostly on the bottom and usually are caught with bait but sometimes strike flies. I've seen schools numbering as much as a hundred lying just under the surface in the Gulf of Mexico off the Louisiana marshes. These school fish rarely take flies, and my best pattern has been a slow-sinking crab. They can often be found tailing on the flats as they root out creatures they eat.

One warm summer evening near Lostman's River in the Ten Thousand Islands of Florida, I was with two of my all-time favorite fishing friends, Ted Juracsik and Flip Pallot. It was getting late, and we had been targeting redfish that were feeding during the falling tide on the oyster bars at the mouth of the river. I was on the bow ready to cast, and Flip was poling when all three of us saw some disturbance in the water tumbling on the down-current side of an oyster bar that would soon be out of the water due to the falling tide.

Flip very quietly moved the boat toward the disturbance. When we got within easy casting distance, I threw a size 2 chartreuse and white Clouser Minnow into the midst of nervous water and allowed it to sink to the bottom. Slow-stripping two or three times, I felt tension on the fly line and pulled back, setting the hook. Nothing happened for a few seconds, but then the hooked fish began to slowly move away with the tide.

I was using an 8-weight rod, and the fish was putting a healthy bend in it. Flip began to pole after the fish as I recovered, lost, and recovered line. After maybe ten minutes, we had the fish beside the boat. Ted held the boat in position while Flip reached down and picked from the water a black drum that probably weighed at least 30 pounds. It was the largest of the species I've caught.

# Threadfin Salmon

# 60

*Polydactylus sheridani*

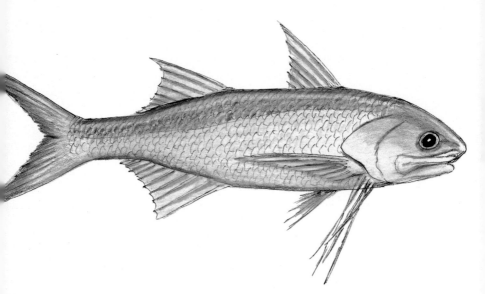

O ne of my favorite fish to catch inshore in Australia's salt waters is the threadfin salmon, which isn't a salmon and doesn't even look like one. It resembles a bonefish—it has a wide tail like a bone but is much heavier in the body. What sets it apart from other fish I've caught are the huge white whiskers or sensory filaments at the base of each pectoral fin that drop down in front of the belly and are apparently used in feeding. So far as I can determine, their range is extreme northern Australia—I have never encountered them anywhere else.

Bathurst Island is a huge island lying a little offshore from northeastern Australia. Rod Harrison and I, along with an Australian television crew, spent a week at the Bathurst Island Fishing Lodge. I believe the island at that time was uninhabited except possibly for a few Aborigines.

A wide tidal river flows past the lodge. The first day we boated upriver a short distance to numerous shallow flats extending well out from shore.

Our boats were shallow-draft skiffs, and the guides began poling in the clear water. I was instructed to put a white Deceiver fly on my 8-weight rod and floating line and to look for threadfin salmon. I had no idea what the devil a threadfin salmon was, but the guide assured me he would show us.

We poled the flat for maybe ten minutes and he suddenly pointed and said, "Cast to that silvery fish about 50 feet away coming toward us." The fish was easy to see against the light brown bottom. I dropped the fly 6 feet in front of it and began a slow retrieve. The fish made several rapid sweeps of the tail and engulfed the fly. Setting the hook, I was unprepared for the hot run it made.

It sped across the flat just like a bonefish, and I could hear the TV cameras whirling. I finally slowed it down and realized more than 50 yards of backing was outside the rod tip. After several runs and retrieves, the fish was at the boat. When Rod lifted it from the water, I was astonished by the long, weird-looking, dangling filaments hanging from behind the head. I thought, I am going to enjoy fishing for them—no matter how crazy they look.

My most cherished memory of threadfin salmon came the next day. One of the TV cameramen was in our boat standing just behind me. The sun was high, the water shallow, calm, and clear, and the bottom light brown—perfect conditions to sight-fish threadfin salmon. We soon saw a fish, and as I began casting, directly behind me I could hear cameras rolling.

Later when we looked at the film we saw it was from the angler's perspective: The camera showed the threadfin salmon heading toward us, the fly line unrolling, and the fly dropping just in front of the fish. The retrieve started, and the fish rushed forward, grabbing the fly, and there was a huge swirl of water and the fish could be seen racing across the flat and finally out of range of the camera.

I don't think I ever saw on film a better example of a presentation from cast to hookup to fish speeding off—for me it was one of the highlights of that great trip.

# Ox-Eye Herring

## 61

*Megalops cyprinoides*

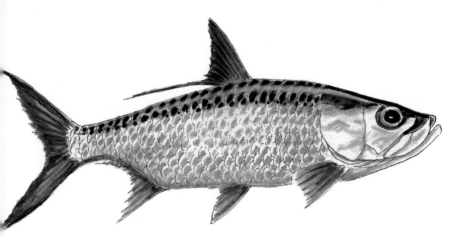

I was making a show about fly-fishing with a TV crew in extreme northern Australia. Part of the trip was to the lightly inhabited Bathurst Island, one of the largest islands in the country off the northeast coast. The huge island is interlaced with rivers, creeks, and hidden bays.

Rod Harrison, senior fishing writer in Australia, and I were casting our flies along the mangrove shorelines, knowing we might catch a variety of species. It had been fun, and we had brought to boat more than half a dozen species.

I made a cast into a small creek coming out of the mangroves and felt a light tap. I set the hook, and a small tarpon erupted into the air and was soon landed. Rod and several of the crewmembers got excited and took photos. I really didn't understand their enthusiasm. This tarpon weighed maybe 3 pounds and was a little more than 2 feet long.

Thousands of such tarpon have been caught in Florida in canals and on the flats, so I was puzzled. It turned out it wasn't a Florida tarpon, but another species that resembled it perfectly called an ox-eye herring. Those with me said it was true trophy. Apparently in Australia they don't get very large and this one was a big one.

# False Albacore

## 62

*Euthynnus alletteratus*,
little tunny

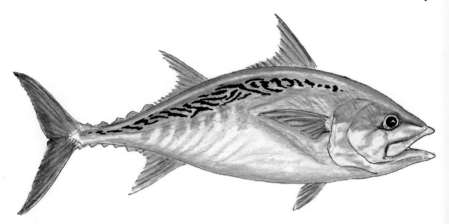

A fishing companion I have shared many trips with, Tom Earnhardt is one of the finest fly casters I know, and he is so upbeat about everything that he keeps me in a state of constant excitement. He called one evening and was all keyed up, urging me to join him for a fishing trip to Harkers Island, North Carolina, where he has a fishing cottage.

"Lefty, you won't believe the fishing. There are acres of false albacore, and no one is fishing them. You just gotta come. Fly into New Bern [North Carolina], and I'll pick you up and we will have a ball," he said.

Three days later we were driving to Harkers Island on the Atlantic coast south of the well-known Outer Banks. There is a huge bay on the west side, but there are a number of inlets reaching the sea.

It was a gorgeous mid-October day, and I recalled I once wrote a column for my newspaper that said, "I wish there were twelve Octobers in a year." For anyone who loves the outdoors in the mid-Atlantic area, there is almost too much to do from hiking, camping, and bird watching to hunting and fishing.

Tom previously told me the albies, as he called them, ranged from about 8 to maybe 18 pounds. They are classified as little tunny, and like the tunas are shaped like a squeezed football. They have that sickle-shaped tail, meaning they will fight like hell when hooked.

Tom developed a fly he said was working well that he called an Alba Clouser, a variation of the Clouser Minnow. It imitated fairly well the small baitfish albies sought. After a quick dawn breakfast at a true Southern-cooking restaurant (my kind of restaurant), we were off to a good start. Tom ran the boat down the channels to the distant Cape Lookout Lighthouse, a tall white structure visible for miles. We stopped immediately in front of the lighthouse and rigged our 8-weight rods with floating lines and his Alba Clousers.

Slowly motoring toward the nearby outlet to the bay, Tom yelled, "Hang on!" and then floored the motor toward a school of albacore leaping above the surface and tearing into a school of baitfish. Stopping the boat just in front of the oncoming albies, we both cast. Within seconds we were hooked up and our reels were singing. These babies were strong and bent our rods danger-ously. We repeated this technique all morning, and Tom and I were acting like two kids.

There were no other fly fishermen around. But there were a number of local people bait fishing for seatrout and other bottom fish. Some watched our antics and just shook their heads as if to say we had to be nuts. When we caught and put the albies back that caused even more disbelief.

Around noon I was tired, and although there were albies jumping out of the water nearby, I ignored them. Tom said, "Okay, it's time for a break." He motored to a dockside restaurant, and we ate a leisurely lunch. By then my batteries had fully charged, and Tom and I were ready for more action, which lasted until we quit late in the afternoon.

I have experienced few such frantic episodes of casting to breaking fish anywhere on the planet. What was even more amazing is no other fly fisher-men were there.

Tom is a sharing person, so the following year maybe a dozen boats joined the fun. Soon the word spread further, and fly fishermen were trailering their boats from as far as Florida and New England. At its peak, Tom and I counted more than 200 boats chasing albies.

After a few years, Donny Jones, the great boat builder, and Tom invited all who came to a pig roast and feast at Tom's fishing home on the island. It was one of the best gatherings of fly fishermen I've ever attended.

The past several years the fishing has decline probably because the bait was scarce, but some still show up and chase the albies, remembering a golden time in our fly-fishing lives. All thanks to Tom Earnhardt.

# Sheefish

# 63

*Stenodus leucichthys,*
tarpon of the North, inconnu

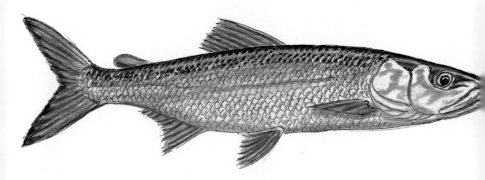

I can honestly say I enjoy catching all kinds of fish with a fly from bluegills to billfish. Only one fish ever disappointed me. I read a number of articles about the sheefish, called the "tarpon of the North," because it resembled somewhat a tarpon and frequently leaped high when hooked.

After several trips to Alaska where I had caught the five species of salmon, Dolly Varden, rainbows, and arctic grayling, I longed to catch the mighty sheefish, sometimes called inconnu. After a wonderful week of fly fishing at the great Bristol Bay Lodge, I made arrangements to fly to the distant Kotzebue, a small village a few miles north of the Arctic Circle, where supposedly the mighty sheefish lived in the local rivers.

In the early 1970s there were only a few unimposing homes in Kotzebue, but I understand now there are several thousand people living there. I inquired and found an Eskimo guide who said he knew where the sheefish were and for a small sum would guide me. At 87 my memory isn't what it used to be, but I think the guide took me to the Kobuk River.

I had 8- and 9-weight rods and a number of Deceivers and other streamer flies. We anchored in a deep pool on a river bend, and I rigged the 9-weight with a lead-core shooting head and a white Deceiver. At the first two locations, I got nothing. At the third deep pool I was slow-stripping when the fly stopped. I set the hook, anticipating a hard-fought battle, and my heart was pounding. Out of the river leaped a silvery fish of maybe 20 pounds.

I put some pressure on the fish, and it came easily toward me, jumping two more times. Within three or four minutes the sheefish was lying exhausted on its side. The guide picked it up, we took a few photos, and then released it.

I was disappointed in the fight, but I have had such things happen with several great gamefish. Once in a while, you get one that acts like it can't fight—or one that will tussle far beyond its actual weight. Tarpon are a good example—I've had 70-pound tarpon fight better than some 100-pounders.

I switched to the 8-weight, a lead-core head, and a white Deceiver. I caught several sheefish that fought about the same as the first. Then I hooked one the guide really got excited about. It was obviously much larger than any so far. Even on the light 8-weight rod I was able after three impressive jumps to quickly bring the big sheefish to the boat. The guide had no scale but estimated it at about 40 pounds.

I have to say I have never landed a 40-pound fish that fought so poorly. Someone asked me when I came home if I finally caught a sheefish and what I thought about it. I answered that you can have about as much fun fighting a wet bath towel.

# Spotted Gar

# 64

*Lepisosteus sp.*,
Florida gar

Some of the most fun I've had with a 6-weight rod and floating line is with the spotted gar. This fish is a survivor, and I am sure it was around a million years ago, judging by its looks. It has a long, yellow, rounded body with large brown spots on the body and fins. The mouth is an extended snout; the interior is hard and boney and filled with many tiny teeth.

I believe that like a tarpon it can obtain oxygen by passing water through the gills or rise to the surface and breath in air. Some of the warm waters of the South where they live hold little oxygen and that's why I think they can take air from above. One of the quickest ways to locate spotted gar is to see them roll like tarpon as they disturb the surface.

I was fishing in northern Florida when I first encountered them. I was having fun with fat and heavy bluegills and other panfish when I saw a long fish roll to the surface. My friend who lived in the area identified it as a gar. I began casting to it, and on the third cast, the fish took the fly. When I set the hook, the tippet was cut.

My friend laughed and said, "You can't catch them. Their mouths are so hard inside and their teeth cut your leader."

That evening in my motel room I decided the next day I was going to catch a gar. I took a 3-inch section of nylon rope and separated the fibers.

Making a thin rope of the fibers about the thickness of a barnburner match, I folded them and whip-finished near the fold to form a sort of hook eye to make a "fly," minus any hook, about 1½ inches long with a lopped eye. They looked good enough that I made half a dozen.

The next day I attached a 40-pound bite leader about a foot long to my leader and tied the fly to it.

Locating several gars rolling on the surface, I cast the hookless fly to one. As soon as the retrieve started, the little fly looked like a small baitfish and there was a savage strike. The gar and I argued over who was going to own this fly, but he soon escaped.

The next gar was not so lucky, and the tiny nylon rope fibers tangled in the teeth so much so that after landing the gar it took considerable time to free all the nylon fibers. Some of the gars weighed nearly 4 pounds and that little 6-weight rod was bent as deep as I ever saw it.

# Cubera Snapper 65

*Lutjanus cyanopterus,*
Cuban dog snapper

This fish I did not catch on a fly but on a plug-casting outfit, but I just gotta tell you about it. It happened back in the 1970s on the Yucatan Peninsula at a lodge called Pez Maya that I understand years ago was swept away in one of the many hurricanes that damage the coast.

Boca Paila is a famous bonefish camp that's been around for decades. Miles south of there is a bridge that spans a waterway on the narrow strip of land that separates the Atlantic Ocean from a huge estuary. But in the 1970s no bridge had been built, and the tide swept in and out of this narrow cut, often at good speed.

The area is not known for numerous big bonefish, but I discovered if you visited the cut just at daylight or nightfall, you'd find large bonefish that came out of the ocean and worked the shallows on the south side close to Pez Maya.

One evening just at dark several large fish swept in on high tide and chased these bonefish, tearing up the water. The next night, armed with a stout plug rod, 15-pound-test line, and a casting lure, I waited. There was a bright moon and my companion and I did not have long to wait.

Soon these big fish were thrashing the water and chasing bonefish. I threw my plug in and was immediately hooked up. The fish tore out of the cut and into the Atlantic at blinding speed. I followed to the ocean surf and began fighting the fish. The reel drag was receiving tough abuse and began to get hot but still smooth.

The fish turned and began running south, and my companion and I followed it. I would gain and lose line, gain and lose line. After a long battle I finally had the fish flopping close to the beach. It was then we both realized it was a big cubera snapper, one of the strongest fish in the sea, and it had a mouth full of sharp teeth.

My barefoot companion had a small hand gaff. I asked him to gaff it and drag it on the beach. As he neared the fish we could hear it snap its mouth open and closed, so he backed off. Finally after much pleading, he waded in, stuck the gaff in the fish's jaw, and heaved it on the beach.

We took some photos and released the fish. Both of us agreed that cubera weighed at least 60 pounds—one of the best catches I ever made on any light tackle.

# King Salmon

# 66

*Oncorhynchus tshawytscha,*
king, tyee, chinook

The king salmon, frequently called a chinook salmon, is the largest of the five salmon species that return to Alaskan rivers to spawn. When fresh from the sea they are silvery on the sides and a blue-green or purple on the back and can weigh more than 60 pounds, although most caught on flies in the rivers average from about 20 to 35 pounds. When they first enter the rivers they are hard fighters, but the longer they remain, while still fun to catch, they don't fight nearly as hard. They gradually change color to a light rose and finally a deep red.

In the late 1970s I was asked to participate in a TV fishing show with Jimmy Dean, the country singer. The filming was to take place on the Pere Marquette River near Baldwin, Michigan.

We stayed in two small motel rooms beside the bank of the stream. Jimmy Dean was 6 foot, 4 inches, and his bed was nearly a foot shorter. The first night his feet hung over the end and kept falling asleep. We corrected that the next night by piling all our luggage at the end of the bed.

Jimmy had a great sense of humor and quick wit. The camera crew was in one room, and Jimmy and I shared the other. The first night we were getting acquainted, and not bragging, Jimmy talked about his properties in Texas and his sausage factory. I asked him, "How many people worked for you, Jimmy?" He thought a minute and answered, "I think about half of them."

It was the start of a fun-filled week.

This area of the Pere Marquette was a fly-fishing-only section. To my dismay I found the first night that we were going to make a TV fishing show with fly rods and Jimmy never used one. The next day I taught him some basic casting—enough for him to get flies to the fish in this rather narrow stream where schools of big king salmon have come out of the lake to spawn. There were places in the river where the bottom was almost covered with them, many around 30 pounds.

I explained how to use a sink-tip line and cast the fly slightly upstream of the salmon and dead-drift it past the fish. It took a while for Jimmy to get the trick of using the fly rod, for he was an old-timer with plug-casting tackle. Finally the fly drifted into a school, and with cameras rolling I yelled, "Set the hook!" A 30-pounder was hooked and turned swiftly downstream. With a snap like a .22 rifle going off, the leader parted. The camera crew was dismayed.

I had turned to Jimmy as soon as the leader broke and found he had clamped the fly line against the rod handle when setting the hook and never released it, allowing the fish to easily break the tippet. I explained how to set the hook and release line to an escaping fish and retied the 12-pound-test tippet.

The second hooked fish broke off when Jimmy clamped again on the fly line, refusing to release it, and we went over the procedure again. After another failure I upped the leader tippet strength to 16-pound-test. Same results. I just couldn't get him to release line when the fish took off. Again it was the same thing. Near the end of the day I used a tippet of 20-pound-test. Now the tippet didn't break, but the hooks straightened. Jimmy hooked maybe ten king salmon, breaking off all of them.

That evening the camera crew chief called me aside and said, "We gotta do something or we're not going to get a show. Can't you think of something?"

I got in the car, drove to a local tackle show, and bought some 30-pound-test line and some carbon-steel saltwater hooks. Back at the motel I tied a few flies.

The next day, with the 30-pound test tied to a saltwater hook dressed for salmon, Jimmy made a cast and hooked up. He still clamped the line against the rod handle, refusing to give line. The big salmon thrashed around, trying to escape. Standing beside him, I looked up and saw the rod bent at an alarming angle just above the rod handle. Thinking the fly rod was going to explode, I made an audible gasp that could later be heard on the show. Instead the rod held, and I finally netted a salmon weighing at least 30 pounds.

The camera crew cheered, and the crew chief said, "We have what we need. Lefty, there is some time left—why don't you fish for a while?" Jimmy waded over, sat on the bank, and began smoking a cigarette. It had been a day and part of a morning before he finally landed a salmon.

Wading out, I drifted a fly through a school, and it was almost like fishing in a hatchery. There was an immediate hookup, and after a few minutes I landed the fish. This was repeated several times, and any novice fly fisherman could have done it.

Sitting on the bank, Jimmy watched as one fish after another was landed. I am sure he was thinking about all of the fish he hooked and allowed to break off. After I caught five or six salmon, Jimmy yelled and I turned to look at him. He was holding up both hands with seven fingers held upright.

"What does that mean?" I asked.

He closed one fist and with the other hand he held upright a single finger. He laughed and answered, "It means a whole week of these."

---

I think the most fun I ever had with kings was when Jim Teeny, who developed the famed Teeny Nymph, and John Randolph, editor of *Fly Fisherman* magazine, were fishing out of Duncan's River Camp on the Kanektok River.

There was a shallow backwater slough with lots of 30-pound kings swimming there. John, Jim, and I waded the slough and sight-fished them. We caught a lot, and I have a photo of the three of us holding up 30-pounders we all landed at the same time.

But the most unusual story I remember involving king salmon occurred on the Nushagak River in the Togiak National Wildlife Refuge. Unlike most rivers fly fishermen enjoy, the Nushagak is a big, deep, fast-flowing river, which may be why it is a prime river to catch king salmon in.

I was staying at Bristol Bay Lodge, one of the finest in all of Alaska. Among the guests was a little guy from Kentucky on his first trip to Alaska to catch salmon. The first night he brought out his "gear," a Zebco cup-faced spinning reel used for light freshwater fishing.

Having fished the huge Nushagak River for king salmon, several of us tried to dissuade him from using this tackle. He told us stories of the big catfish he had caught on this outfit, and even when we showed him our heavy fly tackle, he maintained he could catch the kings on his. The lodge even tried to lend him tackle—no way.

The next day a number of us were flown to the Nushagak, and using boats we fished different areas. That night after returning to the lodge, showering, and joining the others in the main room, our Kentucky friend came in despondent. He had hooked a king salmon with a spoon lure, and when the fish took off, his Zebco drag failed and the entire outfit was jerked from his hands and disappeared into the depths—gone forever.

The lodge lent him regular spinning gear, and he did catch two kings but throughout the week kept lamenting how much he hated losing his favorite fishing outfit.

The last day several of us again fished the Nushagak, and I caught a 35-pounder but lost two to sunken trees on the river bottom. In late afternoon I drifted my lead-core shooting head through a deep pool when there was a gentle strike. After setting the hook there was no sizzling run, just a steady gentle pressure, and I assumed the fly was snagged on one of the many tree branches that were on the river bottom. The guide rowed the boat downstream while I reeled in line. Finally we realized I had hooked another fisherman's monofilament line. Grabbing the line, the guide began to pull the line in the boat hand over hand only to find to our astonishment that on the end was our Kentucky friend's Zebco reel.

After dinner on the last night it was a tradition at Bristol Bay Lodge to award prizes for lots of fun things, such as the biggest fish lost, the fisherman who ran the fastest from a bear, and so on. After all prizes were given Maggie McMillan, the lodge owner, called our Kentucky friend to come forward. He rose with a confused look on his face. Maggie walked in the other room and came out holding his cherished Zebco reel. He had a dumbfounded look on his face, and as he clutched the Zebco outfit to his breast, his smile was bigger than that on a Halloween pumpkin.

If you saw how big, deep, and fast the Nushagak River is and realized he lost his outfit half a mile upstream of where it was snagged, you could not imagine how unusual and lucky we were to snag it for him.

# Smallmouth Bass

# 67

*Micropterus dolomieu,*
smallie, brown bass, black bass, bronzeback

There are many wonderful freshwater species you catch on a fly rod, but my favorite is the smallmouth bass. I suppose it's because it was the first fish I caught on a fly rod. I lived in Frederick, Maryland, and Frederick Valley was lined with small streams that in those days held many smallmouths. The Monocacy River almost circled the town and was home to smallies occasionally weighing more than 4 pounds. The Potomac River, famed for bass in those days, was less than an hour's drive away. Sadly, politicians have allowed massive development in the area. (Frederick was a small town and is now the second-largest city in Maryland.) The need to supply water to the increasing number of residents and businesses has dried up most of the small streams, and the fifty miles of the Monocacy River where we would float and fish from start to mouth is so low that it is no longer possible.

I've been fortunate to enjoy fishing for trout in Europe, South America, and all over the United States, including Alaska, as well as parts of Canada and, best of all, New Zealand. Much as I love trout fishing, if given a choice, I would always opt for smallmouths. The past few years I have been going to Maine, where pristine rivers hold aggressive smallmouths that make fly rodders happy.

Famed outdoor writer Joe Brooks gave me my first fly-casting lesson in the late 1940s, and he left town the next day—I often wondered why. During that lesson Joe taught me the conventional fly-casting method, which was to sweep the rod to 1 or 2 o'clock for the backcast and then bring the rod forward, stopping at 11 o'clock.

I had been catching a lot of smallmouth bass in the local rivers with plug-casting tackle and learned that the longer the casting lure was retrieved, the better the chances of a hookup. The 2 o'clock to 11 o'clock method I soon realized was inefficient, requiring enormous amounts of effort if frequent distance casts were made.

Fly rodding for smallmouth gradually led me to develop the method I have been teaching for decades, in which you take the rod well back, almost parallel to the water in some cases, and then make a forward cast. Bass fishing made me understand that the longer the rod moves through the stroke, the more it aids the caster. Today, millions of fly fishermen use this method, especially in salt water, although many instructors still believe in the brief vertical stroke on the backcast.

From the 1950s through the 1990s the great limestone rivers of the mid-Atlantic area produced fantastic smallmouth bass fishing. I fished many times on the Susquehanna River with one of my best friends, Bob Clouser. He once handed me a fly so ugly that even though he urged me to try it I was reluctant. Finally late in the day I did and it worked.

At the end of that day I returned to Bob's fly shop and excitedly said, "Bob, you really have something here." We began to develop patterns both for fresh and salt water. I realized Bob had developed a remarkable pattern, and after much testing I told Bob, "What are you going to name it?"

"I have no idea," he answered.

"Bob, it should have your name on the fly—if it's alright with you, I am going to call it Clouser's Deep Minnow." Bob agreed.

Soon after I wrote an article for *Fly Fisherman* magazine about the fly, and anglers everywhere started using it. At first it was called Clouser's Deep Minnow, then it was abbreviated to Clouser's Minnow, and now fly fishermen around the world call it a Clouser. Fly fishermen can thank Bob and smallmouth bass for what has become one of the most popular flies ever developed.

My friends and I caught many smallmouths weighing 3 or 4 pounds. Now and then we would weigh an unusually large one that went maybe 4 pounds, 12 ounces or even 4 pounds, 14 ounces—but never a 5-pounder. I enjoy fishing so much that I never set goals on how many or how big were the fish, but in my heart I wanted to catch on a fly rod that damn five-pounder that eluded me for years.

The Potomac River just upstream from Brunswick, Maryland, was a great section to wade. Most of the water is hip deep, filled with limestone ledges and rocks with grass beds along the shore where river shiners were plentiful. On a summer day this was as pleasant a place to fly rod for smallmouths as any I knew.

Over the years I had developed what many call Lefty's Bug. It's a streamlined popping bug that's easy to cast and dressed so the tail almost never fouls during casting. It pops every time you twitch and lifts silently from the surface. I was fishing with two cherished fly-fishing friends, Pete Demchak and Flip Kennedy. Late in the afternoon I cast the bug near a limestone ledge and popped it a few times as it drifted over the ledge. Suddenly the bug was sucked under and I instinctively struck.

"Good God," I yelled to Pete and Flip nearby as the fish of my dreams leaped into the air. Both of my buddies whooped and cheered. The fish was strong, and knowing I really wanted to land it, I slowly backed toward a shallow gravel bar. After four more heart-pounding jumps I had the giant smallmouth in water so shallow Flip was able to pick it up. We weighed it on my accurate scale, and it was 5 pounds, 4 ounces! I had caught my dream fish. Because we were wading, none of us had a camera, but I didn't care. I'll never forget that first smallmouth larger than 5 pounds.

# Blacktip Shark 68

*Carcharhinus limbatus,*
black tip

The backtip and the lemon are the two sharks most commonly encountered in southern Florida and the Caribbean saltwater flats. The lemon is often more aggressive, and I have been threatened several times so that I no longer wade flats where they are seen. The blacktip seems more wary of people, and if they get too close while I'm wading, I have always been able to chase them away by sharply hitting the water with the fly rod immediately in front of them. Often on the flats you encounter a blacktip that is 4 feet or slightly longer, and they can be a lot of fun on a fly rod. When you hook them in the shallows they take off. In the backcountry of the Florida Keys the flats are grass-covered soft mud, and it's awesome to see a hooked blacktip racing across a flat like a runaway snowplow.

When I first started fly fishing for them in the mid-1960s, I made the mistake of retrieving the fly as I would for other species. I soon realized that the mouth of a shark is located well back under the head. When I was working a popping bug the normal way, the shark would eagerly attack, trying to bite it, but the forward part of the head would simply push the bug away. The situation was almost as bad with streamer flies. A shark sweeps its head sideways to grab prey, and once I stopped using popping bugs and retrieved the fly alongside the eye, my success rate climbed.

Many times a shark was hooked in water too shallow to chase with a motor, and it would run so far it was impossible for the guy poling the boat to keep close. What was needed was a reel with a lot of capacity, and my Seamaster and Fin-Nor—at the time the best saltwater reels—did not have that capacity.

Jim Hardy of the famed English Hardy fishing tackle company came to fish tarpon and bonefish with me in Florida. While seeking bonefish on a Keys flats, we encountered a number of good-sized blacktips, and I told Jim about not having enough reel capacity to hang on when a big blacktip took off. Jim said nothing, but about two months later a Hardy reel arrived at my home courtesy of Jim, suggesting maybe this would hold enough line. It did. I have never seen a Hardy reel so large, and it helped me land a number of sharks that might have otherwise gotten away.

Many years later a collector of old reels called and said he had heard I had a lot of reels. I said I did, and he asked me if I had any Hardy reels. I told him I did and described several. When I mentioned the huge reel Jim Hardy had given me, he became very interested. I said, "The problem is it's been around salt water and there's a little corrosion."

"That's okay," he told me and said he would give $800 for it. I was astonished. Wanting to be fair I said, "I should tell you I used an electric metal engraving pen and inscribed my name on the side of it." I was flabbergasted when he said, "Great, I'll give you $1,000 for it." I came right back saying, "Fellow, I got a bunch more with my name on them if you want to buy them." But he was only interested in that Hardy reel.

# Rainbow Trout 69

*Oncorhynchus mykiss,*
'bow

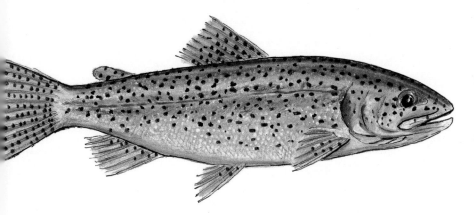

I think it was the very early 1970s when I visited Bristol Bay Lodge while John and Maggie Garry were supervising its construction. The main lodge was nearly finished, and over the years this became one of the premier lodges in all of Alaska. At the time there were few fishing lodges in the region, and during the week I stayed there we never saw another fisherman.

Early during my stay John said to me, "How would you like to fish a river I have never seen anyone fish? I want to check it out to see if it will be good for customers." I jumped at the chance.

The next morning John and his young son Mogie and I were off in John's Beaver floatplane. We flew down the coast of the Bering Sea and entered a wide bay that narrowed at the other end where a river entered. We taxied up the bay to the mouth of the river, John put the Beaver floats against the gravel bar, and we hopped out.

John and I took fly rods and Mogie had a spinning outfit with a wobbling spoon for a lure. We walked up the river a short distance and began casting. Almost immediately we began to catch rainbow trout of all sizes from 14 inches to some that probably weighed 8 pounds—maybe even bigger.

I did not realize we were going to stay so long and had only tied on a Muddler Minnow fly and left my fly gear back at the plane. John wanted to see what was around every bend, so we continued upriver, catching rainbow after rainbow, many large by anyone's standards. I have never before or since caught so many huge rainbows in one day.

After several hours I said to John, "We have to quit," and he asked why. I had started with maybe a 4-foot leader attached to the Muddler Minnow but had to keep snipping off the end near the fly because rainbows were fraying it. I had just caught my last big rainbow and did not have enough leader left to retie. Reluctantly, John decided to return to the plane, and we planned to fly home.

As we approached the plane, we were stunned. Earlier John had taxied up a broad bay perhaps a mile wide at the mouth. The bay was now empty of water and our plane sat on the dry gravel bar! John explained that in this part of the world, an 18-foot tide was not unusual. "You know a lot about tides," he said. "When do you think it will come back?"

I answered, "Tides usually change every six hours, so we probably will have to wait almost six hours before we can get out of here."

Seven hours later the bay was still empty, and I told John, "I hate to say this, but in a few places in the world there is what is called a diurnal tide where there is just one high and one low tide a day. I think that's what's happening here. That means we are going to be stuck for a good many hours."

About 200 yards down the beach lay the body of a huge walrus with the head missing. John said probably some Eskimos illegally killed the walrus, chopped off the head for the ivory, and allowed the body to wash ashore. I was told a walrus weighs 3,000 pounds, and that walrus on the beach was the size of a big living-room sofa. Down over the bank came a huge Kodiak bear that began to tear away at the walrus, making us very uncomfortable.

The only thing we had to defend ourselves was John's .44 Magnum pistol, hardly the weapon to use against such a large bear. To complicate matters, another big Kodiak bear appeared, and the two began to growl and snarl at each other—even though there was enough meat for ten bears. When the two bears began to fight each other, we decided that pistol was not much protection and we should hide in the plane.

By now it was dark. In this part of the world in June there is enough light at night to barely read a newspaper—it just never gets totally dark. The two bears had stopped fighting. About one o'clock in the morning we heard what sounded like a roaring river rapids. Peering out of the plane windows we saw a vertical wall of water rushing up the bay. Within less than an hour, the entire bay was filled and John took off.

Our destination was Lake Aleknagik—as I remember it's about 13 miles long with the Bristol Bay Lodge at the upper end. It had been a too-long day, and I was looking forward to a good sandwich and a bed.

John found Lake Aleknagik and began circling. I could see the lodge in the dim light, but John wasn't landing; he was circling over the lake. "John, why in the hell don't you land?" I asked. He answered, "I'm looking for a duck."

"Why the hell are you looking for a duck?" I growled. John explained that the lake was so calm it resembled a mirror and in the poor light he didn't know where the surface was. If he saw some ducks swimming, they would ripple the lake surface and he could land. We never found the duck, so John explained that we would go to the far end of the lake and he would slowly let the plane down. When we hit the water, we might bounce a little, but we would then taxi to the lodge.

We began a slow descent toward the lodge, and I anxiously looked down at the calm surface. Honest—moments before we landed the lake looked the same as it did when we were obviously well above it. Once the floats touched the water, John taxied rapidly to the camp where Maggie waited with hot coffee and sandwiches.

When I think of rainbow trout, I often recall that fantastic fishing on that river, the unbelievable rush of the incoming tide, and John looking for a duck so we could land in that dim northern light.

# Lookdown

70

*Selene vomer*, horsehead

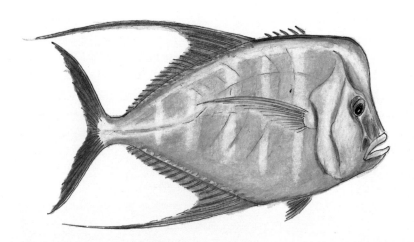

Perhaps of all the fish I have caught on a fly the lookdown is the weirdest-looking. The body is so thin it looks as if a car ran over it. What distinguishes it is not only its compressed body but where the eyes are located. The mouth is at the very bottom but the eyes are well above, and to see anything other than in front and above, the fish has to look down—hence the name.

I lived in South Miami from the mid-1960s to early 1970s. My son Larry and I liked to fish at night under the lighted bridges, especially in Biscayne Bay where the illumination attracted baitfish, snook, baby tarpon, and lookdowns. It wasn't allowed, but we would tie the boat to one of the wooden structures on either side of the boat channel and walk to the uptide side where we could see the various fish feeding on baitfish, drifting shrimp, and crabs.

A big lookdown might weigh a pound. Few I ever saw did, but with a 4-weight rod and a small baitfish imitation, you could hook the aggressive lookdowns and with their wide, flat bodies they would put a hurtin' on a light fly rod. It was fun! Some say you can eat them, but their bodies are so compressed I don't think you would get much meat off one.

# Coho

## 71

*Oncorhynchus kisutch,*
silver salmon, silvers

I made numerous trips to Alaska beginning in the late 1960s. There are five species of salmon spawning in these rivers, and once I caught silver salmon—locally called silvers or coho—they became my favorite even though the king salmon is much larger.

If you are not familiar with the salmon runs in Alaska, you may not realize that there are no adult salmon in these rivers except during their summer runs. The adults come in prodigious numbers, and once they spawn they die. They have to because there is little protein food in the rivers and if the parents did not sacrifice themselves, there would be little for their young to survive on.

In the Bristol Bay region of Alaska—about the size of the state of Ohio— the coho runs usually begin in mid-August and last for several weeks, with the bulk of the returning fish filling the rivers during the first two weeks.

Fresh from the sea, cohos are bright silver with dark blue backs and take flies readily. They jump and fight well, and the average size is between 8 and 14 pounds, although they can reach almost 20 pounds in rare cases. They are a perfect fly-rod fish you can catch on a 7- or 8-weight rod. After being in the river a while, they change color: their sides become bright red, heads bluish green, and the male's jaws become hooked with pronounced teeth.

There are times the rivers become so choked with them that I use a bend-back fly (a weedless pattern). A conventional fly retrieved through the schools will foul-hook many, something I hate to do. I recall staying at a spike camp (tent camp) years ago on the Togiak River and there were so many cohos in the pool in front of us that I caught 24 cohos on 28 casts.

But when I think of coho I vividly remember just one. The guide had gone upriver in the boat to retrieve my two companions, and I was alone. I had caught several cohos. Another was hooked and jumped several times not more than 40 feet from me. Out of the brush rushed a giant Kodiak bear (a big one will stand 8 feet on its hind legs) that grabbed my salmon. I swept the rod back to dislodge the salmon, and the bear turned to me and snarled. I dropped the rod and fled into the bushes, making my way upstream as quickly as possible. Ten minutes later I heard the jet motor on the guide's boat as he returned. Wading into the river, I stopped him and explained what happened. The guide, being an old hand, suggested we just stay there a while to give the bear time to have his lunch. Half an hour later we came downriver to the sandbar where I had been fishing. The bear was gone, and my rod lay on the bank where I dropped it. It was retrieved, and we headed to the floatplane and back to the lodge.

# African Pompano

# 72

*Alectis ciliaris,*
threadfin, Cuban jack

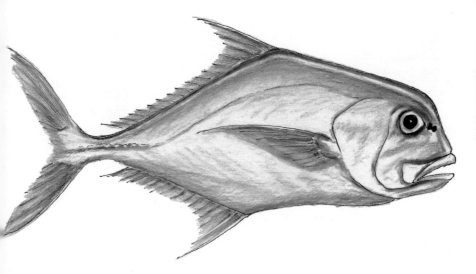

I've been lucky to catch eight African pompano on fly rods, but two of them stand out. I am not sure why they call them "African" pompano. They live in almost all seas where the temperature stays warm, not just near Africa. And I don't think they are in the pompano family—instead they are closely related to the jack family, and mature fish are often thought to be jacks. Africans are built like jacks, hard-muscled with a sickle tail. Hook one of more than 20 pounds and you'll have a helluva fight on your hands.

I was fishing a 3-inch Deceiver fly near Cosgrove Light west of Key West and cast to some nervous water. I had a gentle take and set the hook with my 8-weight rod. The fish was quickly brought to boat. I had never seen any fish like it. It resembled a small jack crevalle, but stringing back from both ends of the dorsal and pectoral fin were dark streamers longer than the fish. These "filaments" were exceptionally flexible and did not seem to impede the fish, which could not have weighed 4 pounds. I gently released it.

It was when I got home and looked in my fish species book that I learned I had caught a small African pompano. The book indicated the long filaments were typical of the young, and it is thought those filaments might discourage large prey fish. Once the fish gets a little larger, it loses those filaments, although two I caught still had partial filaments.

Another African pompano I did not catch, but Dan Blanton, one of my best fishing buddies, did.

As I recall it was in the 1970s, and we were staying at the Turneffe Island Lodge. The Turneffe Islands are sort of misnamed, since there are few actual solid islands. Lying about 30 miles offshore east of Belize is a long, wide string of mangrove standing in the water with an occasional island of solid land. Located on the southern end was our lodge—for years the only fishing camp there.

The Turneffes are known for their bonefishing, and Dan and I caught plenty. In those days before natives began netting them, they were around in incredible numbers. To the west of the Turneffes the shallows extended about a half-mile and then deepened over a coral reef.

We both enjoyed fishing lead-core shooting heads and dropping flies deep—never knowing what would grab them. The third day it was dead calm, so we asked the guide to take us to the reef. The small bonefish skiff was safe because if the wind came up, we could quickly come inshore.

Dan and I were having a great time catching snappers, grouper, and a mixed bag of species off the reef. Apparently no one had ever fished flies there. After maybe two hours I heard Dan grunt and saw his rod bent dangerously. We knew he was into something different and good. Dan fights fish well, and yet the battle took quite a while.

In the air-clear water we could finally see down deep to a fish with a broad silvery body. Gradually Dan brought the fish to the boat. It was an African pompano, maybe 25 or 30 pounds, the biggest African I had seen taken on a fly. We took photos and then released it. It was the fish that made our trip.

# Sockeye Salmon 73

*Oncorhynchus nerka,*
red salmon, kokanee

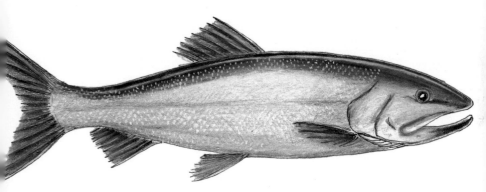

Jim Teeny is a fishing machine and one of my best friends. His wife, Donna, is perhaps one of the top ten fly-fishing ladies in our country. Together they make a team that fish should be aware of. I joined them to fish the Kanektok River, and we stayed at the famous Duncan's River Camp.

It is a joy to watch Jim fishing. As he moves from one location to another, you would think he is sneaking up on a deer. When close to fish, he hunkers down, knees bent, to get a low profile that reminds me of a great blue heron stalking its dinner.

Over the years I fished Alaska I caught many sockeye salmon and believe that for their size and when fresh from the sea, they fight as well or harder than any of Alaska's salmon. I think they more closely resemble the Atlantic salmon than any of the Pacific species. The belly is white, and the sides gradually turn silver and then pale blue with a dark back—much like an Atlantic.

I had been frustrated sometimes when fishing for sockeyes. I found them sometimes more difficult to catch than the four other species. Often a brightly colored orange or pink fly resembling a salmon egg, or a pale cream material tied to a hook to look like a piece of decaying salmon flesh, was needed. On another occasion a plastic bead looking just like a salmon egg worked—and sometimes they refused all we offered.

I mentioned this to Jim the first day as we jet-boated to our first fishing hole on the river. "Don't worry, Lefty," he said. "I have the flies that will work. I guarantee you." I said nothing but remained to be convinced, hoping Jim was right.

Many years ago Jim invented a fly tied with only a single feather. It was so unusual he was able to patent it. Word gradually got around and people demanded to buy them, so he went into business and the fly-fishing world learned about the famed Teeny Nymph. With that one pattern Jim has caught dozens of species in both fresh and salt water.

Jim gave me a box of the flies and I tied one on. On the second drift I hooked a sockeye. I have never hooked as many sockeyes as I did with Jim's nymphs, and over the years it has become my favorite pattern for them—and many other species.

# Flounder

## 74

*Paralichthys* sp., *Pseudopleuronectes* sp.,
flatfish, winter flounder, summer flounder, fluke

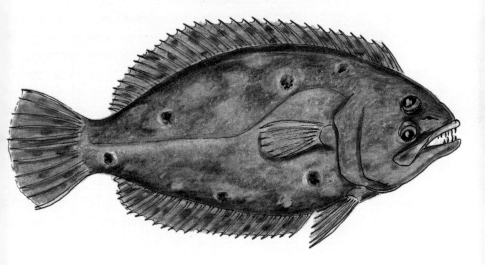

I have never been wild about eating most saltwater fish. But those with white meat that I really enjoy are dolphin, grouper, snapper (especially hog snapper), flounder, and best of all, the coral trout that looks like a grouper that we caught in New Guinea. They are so good to eat that I never saw one caught that was released.

I live in Maryland, and my choice eating fish is the flounder. It is the one species that I bring home if I'm successful when I fly-fish. Sinepuxent Bay is a shallow body of water lying on the west side of Ocean City, Maryland, connected to the Atlantic Ocean by a cut at Ocean City opened years ago by a strong hurricane.

During the summer months the flounder enter the bay to feed on the schools of baitfish. Flounder are ambushers. They have the ability to blend perfectly with the bottom. After locating an ambush spot they burrow their flat bodies into the sand or silt with only the eyes and mouth extending above. The hapless baitfish swims by and like a rattlesnake striking, the flounder sweeps upward, grabbing the baitfish so fast it's hard to follow.

Because the water is so shallow, a floating line and 10-foot leader are all you need. Since most of the food flounders pounce on is baitfish, Clousers in white with a chartreuse top and just a bit of Flashabou work well.

Because flounders bury in the mud or silt to ambush bait, the most effective retrieve is to keep the fly close to the bottom. There is no doubt when flounders take flies that they strike hard and usually hook themselves if you are retrieving with a tight line. For such a flat fish, they put up a surprisingly good fight.

The flounder is not a glamour fish, but it is the one species that I try to catch to eat.

# Blue Runner

# 75

*Caranx crysos*,
hardtail jack, runner, blue jack

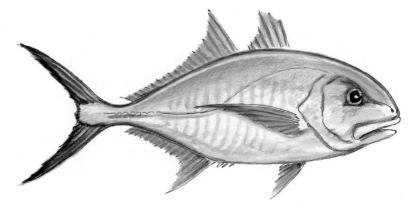

The blue runner is a prime bait anglers use for all sorts of saltwater game-fish. One reason fishermen desire them is they are so hardy. Even in a live well that's lacking some oxygen, they seem to do well.

They are splendid kite baits to tease fish from deep down. You fly a kite away from the boat with a line dangling down and at the end hook a baitfish, allowing it to struggle on the surface and attract sailfish, grouper, kingfish, and other predatory species.

One of my favorite methods using blue runners is when fly fishing over a submerged wreck. The mate hooks a blue runner in the back and lowers it to the surface where it begins to splash, drawing up all sorts of species that hide in the wreck below. When they get to the surface and try grabbing the blue runner, the mate repeatedly pulls it away. This enrages the predator fish. When the mate thinks they are properly teased, he pulls the blue runner from the water, and the fisherman casts his fly.

The fun for me is catching the blue runners. We use an 8-weight rod and leader to which a number of small weighted flies are attached. Blue runners like to hang around channel buoys and similar structure. You cast and retrieve erratically, and if blue runners are there, they jump on the flies. It's a ball getting them in.

# Arctic Char

76

*Salvelinus alpines*,
blueback char

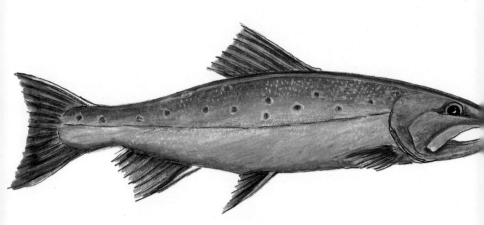

I began fly-fishing Alaska in the late 1960s and made numerous trips to the vast state, but I especially like the Bristol Bay area. In talking to others who've caught all five species of salmon that spawn there, many agree the arctic char for its size fights hardest.

It somewhat resembles a brook trout but lacks the worm track markings on the back and has white-tipped fins. Depending on where it is caught, the color can be a little different; in some areas the flesh is almost red and in other waters it is light pink. I suspect it has to do with the food they eat. In most of Alaska, char rarely grow to more than 10 pounds, but the real trophies live in far northern Canada.

One of the things visiting fishermen most enjoy about Alaska is the shore lunches. You catch a few fish just before stopping and fillet them. The guide builds a fire while you rest on a sandbar or the soft tundra moss, and from out of nowhere gulls arrive. The guide begins by slicing potatoes. A huge frying pan is placed on the fire and the potatoes are dumped in, followed by slices of fresh-caught fish. Drinking coffee from a pot sitting in the fire and eating crispy fried potatoes with fried fresh-caught fish is better than any $100 meal in a fancy restaurant. For me the arctic char is the tastiest of all Alaska's species.

The fastest and most fun arctic-char fishing I ever had was when I was staying at Bristol Bay Lodge, which sits on the shore of Lake Aleknagik. A ten-minute boat ride down the lake, the Agulowak River enters. If you hit it right, the arctic char concentrate in huge numbers just off the river mouth where the water drops deeply into the lake. They feed on the tiny salmon coming down the river in their hazardous run for the ocean.

You can often hook a char on every third cast using a sinking line and tiny streamer flies that are white on the bottom and green on top. There are few times when I simply get tired fighting fish that average 4 to 7 pounds with a 7- or 8-weight rod, but these char will do you in.

# Almaco Jack

# 77

*Seriola rivoliana,*
Almaco

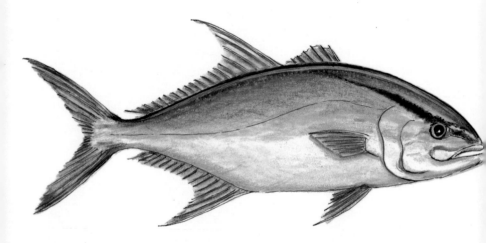

he Almaco jack resembles the amberjack but doesn't get nearly as large. It has the tapered body of a jack and it is all muscle, with a sickle-shaped tail that means you are in for fight once you hook such a fish. They are usually found on deep reefs or around wrecks, and not many are taken by fly rodders for that reason.

Capt. Boyd Gibbons of Bermuda took me to Challenger Bank about 7 miles off the island's coast in the mid-1970s. Traveling over thousands of feet of Atlantic Ocean, you come to Challenger Bank, a huge uprising from the sea floor to within a hundred or so feet of the surface. On the way out I mentioned that I had always wanted to catch an Almaco jack, and Boyd assured me there was a good chance that day.

The wind was up a bit and the sea a bit rough as we anchored in about 150 feet of water on the bank, if I recall. Since I was using a floating fly line and a 6-inch Deceiver fly, I wondered how we would ever get to those Almaco jacks down below.

I am always learning something new about fishing, and Boyd pulled out a magic trick I had never seen. He had a wire mesh cylinder about 6 inches in diameter with one end sealed with mesh wire, to which was attached a long parachute cord. The other end was open.

"This is how we are going to get you your Almaco jack," Boyd said. I was mystified. A favorite chum food in Bermuda is the hogmouth fry—sometimes called the Bermuda anchovy. It is a 2- or 3-inch-long silver baitfish. Boyd's mate packed the cylinder full of the dead fry. While holding on to the parachute cord, he threw the mesh cylinder open-end-first toward the sea.

I had not noticed before, but the parachute cord had a series of knots along its length. As the mate allowed the cylinder to rapidly sink into the depths I noted he was counting the knots as they slid through his hands. Because the cylinder was descending rapidly with the open end downward, all of the chum remained in the cylinder. When the cylinder hit the bottom, the mate announced that the number of knots that passed through his hands was six. The knots were spaced 25 feet apart, so that meant the cylinder now lay on the bottom of Challenger Bank 150 feet below.

The mate gave a quick yank upward on the parachute cord, which flushed the contents of hogmouth fry on the bottom. Hand over hand he brought the wire mesh cylinder up and refilled it. This time he allowed the cylinder to only descend four knots, or 100 feet, flushing it and then bringing it back to the surface. He did this twice more, and each time the cylinder was flushed higher in the water column. Finally he threw several handfuls of the fry on the surface.

To my astonishment, behind the boat all sorts of fish began to appear. Apparently they had been following the flow of chum from the depths to boatside. Boyd was right; several Almaco jacks were taking the dead fry the mate continued to throw on the water. Noting that none of the fry were more than 3 inches, I switched the Deceiver to a 3-inch simple white bucktail, tossed it maybe 15 feet to a cruising Almaco jack, and got an immediate hookup. Line sizzled through the guides, and the drag gave down into the backing. I began to really put pressure on this tough fighting fish and finally after a hard battle landed what Boyd though was a 20-pound Almaco jack.

Whenever I think of that species I think about the unique method of bringing fish from the deep bottom all the way to the surface with a simple mesh cylinder, a parachute cord, and a lot of dead hogmouth fry.

# Gafftopsail Catfish

# 78

*Bagre marinus,*
sail cat

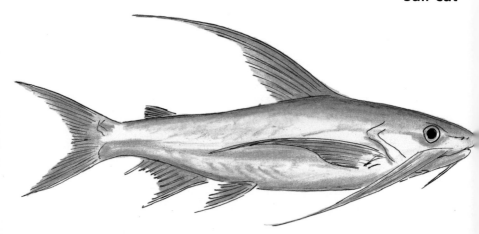

The most unpleasant fish I ever caught is the gafftopsail catfish. If you are not familiar with saltwater species, you would associate catfish with fresh water, but the gafftopsail is a saltwater cousin that looks much like the channel catfish found in fresh water.

Most catfish feed on the bottom of a lake or river, but the gafftopsail hunts throughout the water column and is swift enough to catch much of its prey. They readily take 2- to 3-inch flies and when hooked put up a good fight for their size. I don't know how large they get, but the heaviest one I ever caught was about 3 pounds.

Catches are almost always accidental since no fly fisherman wants to hook and land a gafftopsail catfish for two reasons: Their bodies are coated in a heavy slime that often fouls the leader and fly and is difficult to remove from the hands if they are picked up. What's worse is that they have venomous spines, which when touched inject a poison similar to a bad bee sting.

I've enjoyed catching every species on a fly from bluegills to billfish—except the gafftopsail catfish.

# Sheepshead

## 79

*Archosargus probatocephalus,*
convict fish, bait-stealer

The sheepshead is a prolific fish that is found in the shallows along the Atlantic coast as far north as Long Island and around the Gulf of Mexico to the Mexican border and maybe into Mexico.

Sheepshead are shaped much like bluegills but have heavy scales, muscular bodies, and teeth that are so strong they feed on small clams, mussels, and other creatures. They are found near rock piles and pilings supporting bridges and piers, but fly fishermen encounter them mostly on the flats. Their bodies are pale gray with several contrasting dark vertical stripes, and they are often called convict fish. The average size is 2 to 4 pounds, but they can grow much larger.

When I first moved to Miami in the 1960s and began fishing the flats in Florida Bay and the Keys, I wanted to catch every species I saw. Frequently I would encounter sheepshead meandering the flats searching for food. I tried different retrieves with many of the regular flies that worked on small jack crevalle, snappers, and other species close to the sheephead in size. They ignored every presentation—worse, they often didn't spook but just ignored my offerings.

If you are a fisherman, you know that after trying so hard to catch a fish that ignores you, it gets kind of personal. You are not concerned if it's not necessarily a huge fish but only that it's one you wanted to catch, so I never gave up. I read about what the sheepshead ate and its other characteristics. One scientist wrote they ate shrimp and crabs. I tied several shrimp and crab patterns—still no luck. I began to think they just wouldn't take a fly, so I finally conceded defeat—but it rankled me.

Years later I fished several times with Del Brown, an old fishing companion, and watched him catch permit on his now-famous Merkin crab pattern.

I remembered what that scientist said about sheepshead eating crabs, so I made several thumbnail-size Merkins. The next time I was on a flat, I searched for sheepshead and saw one cruising. The fly dropped just in front of him, and I began crawling it along the bottom. I was holding my breath. Damned if that fish didn't just swim away. I decided to try another sheepshead nearby. This time I threw the fly 4 feet in front of the fish and allowed it to sit on the bottom. The fish slowly worked to within a few inches of the fly, and I was so interested in its action that I failed to retrieve the still crab. The sheepshead tilted down and grabbed my crab fly, and I was so astounded I almost forgot to set the hook.

When I landed that 2-pounder I was as tickled as if it were a 10-pound bonefish. I tried the same technique on three other sheepshead that day but they ignored it. Over the years I have caught enough of them to know if you are persistent and the sheepshead sees that motionless crab, you have a chance to hook and land one. I still find them to be one of the most difficult fish to fool with a fly.

# Bowfin

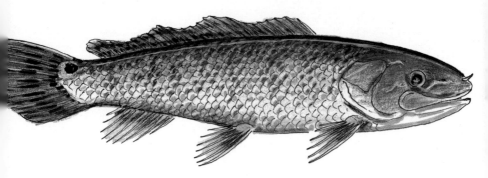

## 80

*Amia calva,*
mudfish, mud pike, dogfish,
swamp muskie, lawyer

Paul Crum is a lifelong fishing friend I grew up with in Frederick, Maryland. At the time, it was a small town of maybe 12,000 people in central Maryland close by the Blue Ridge Mountains. The Potomac and Monocacy rivers were nearby, and we used either a canoe or a johnboat to fish mainly for smallmouth bass.

We also enjoyed many days wading the smaller tributaries with ultralight tackle and 4-pound-test lines casting tiny Rapalas, a rubber lure called a Floppy, and other miniature plugs and small spinners. The creeks were filled with aggressive sunfish and smallmouth bass to about 2 pounds. We spent many pleasant hours wet-wading together and taking turns casting into fishy pockets of water.

In 1964 I moved to Florida to manage the Miami MET Tournament. I bought a flats skiff and with my son Larry began fishing the Everglades and the Florida Keys. Paul and I frequently talked about the fishing, and I finally convinced him to come share it for a few days with me. We fished the flats and over some wrecks, and finally the last day we took my canoe to the

**159**

Everglades. In those days sugar farmers had not robbed the Glades of their water, and it was a fisherman's paradise.

Being bass fishermen, that was our main target, and we caught several dozen. These were the Florida strain of bass with backs as shiny as new black cars. We were walking along the L-37 Canal bank casting into the 10-foot-deep water and having a great time.

Paul was 75 yards from me when he set the hook and began yelling, "Lefty, I got the world's record bass—come help me." I dropped my rod and raced to him. Judging the way the rod was bent and the pressure Paul was putting on that fish, it had to be a real trophy. I crawled down the bank and got ready to net the big bass when Paul got it close enough.

Finally the fish rose, and as I dipped the net toward it, I was amazed. It was the largest bowfin I had seen, at least 10 pounds!

Bowfins are one of the few freshwater fish that have survived through the centuries. Scientist say they were around during the Jurassic period, and they can live in water low in oxygen by rising to the surface and breathing in air. They look prehistoric and ugly with a large dorsal fin that runs more than half the body length, and I am sure they are not good to eat.

There was no camera handy, so we released the fish. Paul was a bit disappointed that it wasn't a record fish, but it sure was the biggest bowfin I've seen caught.

# Cichlids

## 81

## Family Cichlidae

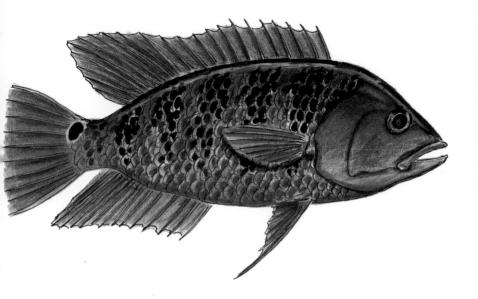

There are more than 1,000 species of cichlids. They come in a variety of colors, shapes, and lengths, and most are the size of panfish with a few growing a bit larger. Many are raised in home aquariums. Some species feed on algae; other species will eat anything they can get in their mouths.

The cichlid family is huge and includes the famous peacock bass, which can grow to more than 20 pounds, and the popular tilapia, which is now commercially raised as a food fish and found in restaurants around the world.

The lower Everglades of Florida has many canals and dirt roads laced through it that were dug in a futile effort to drain the Glades. These canals formerly harbored baby tarpon weighing up to maybe 12 pounds, the Florida strain of largemouth bass, snook, and several species of sunfish—some of the bluegills weighed more than a pound, and I've caught bass, tarpon, and snook that exceeded 10 pounds on various types of tackle.

It was great fun to drive the remote dirt roads bordering the canals and catch fish with either an 8-weight fly rod for bass, tarpon, and snook or a 4-weight rod for panfish. We quickly learned baitfish would gather where the tiniest trickle of water fed into a canal and of course the bass, tarpon, snook, and panfish would follow.

Sadly, this has all changed. Steve Kantner, the Land Captain, specialized for years in guiding this area. With a canoe on top of his car, he would drive many of these little-known and visited dirt roads, and his anglers would fish either from the road or from his canoe.

Steve took me there several years ago, and I was shocked. That day we saw no baby tarpon, only two small snook, and just a few bass. What we did see were cichlids everywhere. Steve explained that apparently people had them in their home aquariums, and when they wanted to get rid of them they simply dumped them into the Everglades. They have become so prolific that it's rare to catch a panfish—apparently sunfish can't compete.

It is fun with a 4-weight fly rod to fish for cichlids—you don't know what color, size, or subspecies you'll catch. But I'd trade all of this to have those canals back to what they used to be.

# Atlantic Bonito 82

*Sarda sarda*,
Boston mackerel, skipjack

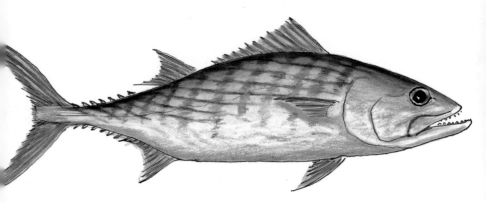

This is a hot little fish rarely heavier than 10 pounds—but once you hook one on a fly rod, you feel like you are hooked to an underwater rocket. Maybe it's a good thing they don't grow bigger. They roam in schools, so find one and you have a chance to offer your flies to a number of them.

I believe scientists classify them as mackerels, but I think they resemble tuna. They have the same body shape, and when grasped, the firm muscles are as unyielding. Like tunas, they have that sickle tail.

Their favorite food is small baitfish such as anchovies, smaller alewives, menhaden, etc. Fly fishermen cruise the waters looking for bonito, which push baitfish toward the surface and then shoot from underneath and grab them. Like albacore, they often leap out of the water a short distance before falling back. Fishermen will always recognize skyrocketing bonito once they see them.

It's chase and cast, chase and cast, and the action is frenetic. A school is sighted and one or more fly fishermen stand ready to cast while the boatman determines the direction the bonito are chasing bait. He tries to get the boat in front of them so that the fishermen can cast to the approaching fish.

Sometimes it works and sometimes it does not. Then the whole procedure is repeated. Often after half an hour or less everyone just sits down to take a breather. It is some of the best fun you can have inshore with a fly rod.

Perhaps my most memorable bonito catch was because I had brought the wrong tackle. Bonito when hooked don't run out of sight, but for maybe 50 or so yards they streak through the water, requiring a light but smooth drag.

On this trip I was in the boat headed to my guide's favorite spot as I dug into my bag to rig for the day. Removing the reel from the neoprene protective bag I stared in horror. By mistake I had picked up the wrong bag, and in my hand was an old freshwater reel, a Shakespeare Russell Model Number 1895. The reel carried enough backing capacity because of its 3½-inch diameter, which held about 150 yards of Dacron. But it had just a simple click drag that prevented the spool from overrunning if line was stripped from it too fast. Luckily the handle side of the spool was smooth. Rigging the outfit, I said nothing to my guide because I didn't want him to think I was dumb enough to bring such a reel.

We arrived at the chosen location, and within ten minutes we saw a few bonitos leaping from the surface as they chased their prey. I was at the bow as the guide raced the boat to get ahead of them. When we were in position he killed the motor, and I dropped the small Surf Candy fly in front of the school and began stripping fast. I hooked up almost immediately, and the bonito took off in its characteristic speedy escape run. Pressing my fingertip against the smooth surface of the reel spool, I was able to control the fish, but that damned small handle banged my fingers until I discovered how to apply pressure and avoid the spinning devil. Normally with a smooth drag it's no trick to land the bonito, but with this reel every fish was a challenge.

# Striped Marlin

## 83

*Tetrapturus audax,*
stripe

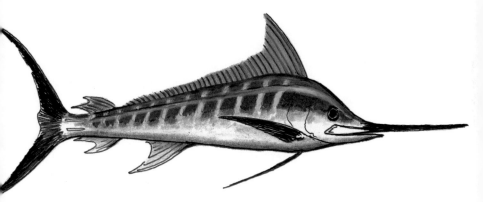

T he striped marlin is a beautiful fish that can weigh several hundred pounds. It resembles other marlin, with a white belly slighter darker on the side and a series of interrupted vertical dark blue stripes (hence the name) with an iridescent blue back and sharp dorsal fin. The bill is very solid and is often used to stun prey.

I first became interested in them during the 1960s by associating with Dr. Web Robinson, who along with his wife Helen and Capt. Lefty Regan developed the modern method of teasing fish to the boat and then removing the teaser and substituting a fly or lure. Lefty was a good friend of mine—we fished together often—and he said their earliest work teasing fish to the boat was with striped marlin in the Sea of Cortez.

Years later I had a chance to fish the Sea of Cortez with Lew Jewette, who was charged with managing the Scientific Anglers part of the massive 3M complex. We flew to La Paz. Upon arriving, an older man got out of his two-engine plane and walked over to ask if we had the latest newspapers and sports pages. It was Bing Crosby, who for years spent a great deal of time there.

The Sea of Cortez is a long narrow body of seawater bordered on one side by mainland Mexico and to the west by the slim Baja Peninsula. The incredibly clear waters are rich in aquatic life, including huge schools of various baitfish to feed various species. At the top of the line is the striped marlin. We encountered dorado everywhere we cruised as well as several species of tuna and hard-fighting roosterfish.

After listening to all of the tales of Doc Robinson and Lefty Regan, I was eager to catch a striped marlin. We boarded a 24-foot local boat equipped with a powerful diesel engine. The captain ran less than a mile to what he called a bait barge--the first I had seen. It was a smaller boat with a deep floating net beside it. The net swarmed with hundreds of small fish. Our mate bought maybe two dozen of the baitfish and put them in our boat's live well.

While underway, the mate rigged a hookless trolling skirt with one of the baitfish attached so the skirt surrounded the small fish. Having listened to Doc and Lefty many times, I recognized this as a teaser.

After a short run, the captain slowed the boat, and the mate lowered the skirted fish into the water, allowing it to stream behind the boat. Aware of what to do, I had a bucket at my feet holding a good bit of fly line. The skirted baitfish was dancing in and out of the water in the 2-foot waves when suddenly from the flying bridge the captain yelled and I saw a dorado grab the baited lure. The mate yanked it away and began rapidly retrieving it as the dorado gave chase. When the lure was within 15 feet of the boat, the mate, using a long rod, yanked it from the water. The dorado—maybe 20 pounds—was searching for it when I dropped the sailfish fly in front of it and was immediately hooked to the dorado, which began tail-walking across the ocean. I was having a ball.

After the fish was landed, the captain stopped the boat and came down the ladder to talk to me. His English was fair and I understood that if I wanted to catch a striped marlin I shouldn't throw the fly at any dorados. I felt a bit chastened, but I agreed.

During the next two hours dorados attacked the baited lure so often that twice the baits became so mangled they had to be replaced. I understood the captain's wishes, but I sure wanted to throw to those fish.

Just after lunch, the captain got really excited and I saw my first striped marlin. It came out of nowhere and smacked the baited lure with its bill. The mate immediately began reeling in. The marlin chased it, got it in its mouth, and I guess tasted the bait. The mate yanked it out of the fish and reeled closer.

The marlin went berserk and colors rippled over its body almost like a neon sign. The mate had told me when that happened to be ready—I was!

When he had teased the marlin to within 20 feet of the boat, he yelled, "Now!" and yanked the baited lure away. The boat stopped and I cast just to the other side of the fish. The marlin turned toward the popping bug-and-streamer fly combination and took it. I stripped struck using my body and my arm. I have to tell you I never saw line go so fast through the rod guides as when that fish tried to get out of town.

It was in and out of the water a number of times as I lost, regained, lost, and regained line. What an aerial display for a fly fisherman! The captain handled the boat perfectly, and within 15 minutes we had the huge fish alongside. We didn't pick it out of the water and the mate removed the fly. Both agreed the fish was about 125 pounds. The mate grasped the bill, holding the marlin just under the surface as the captain slowly moved forward forcing fresh water over the marlin's gills. Within two minutes the revived fish tore from the mate's hands and disappeared into the depths.

I silently thanked Doc and Helen Robinson and Capt. Lefty Regan for developing this incredibly exciting teasing method for catching fish with a fly. I'll never forget how that marlin lit up as it tried to get that teaser.

# Bermuda Chub

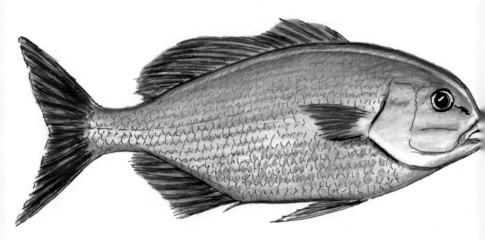

## 84

*Kyphosus sectator*,
butter bream, sea chub

B ermuda is one of the greatest offshore fly-fishing places close to the
United States. Sitting on the eastern edge of the Gulf Stream and a little
more than an hour's plane ride from New York, it offers fantastic fishing. There are two large flattop mountains just a few miles off the coast that
rise from the deep ocean to within 200 feet of the surface, attracting all sorts of
local fish as well as those roaming the open seas.

Usually fishermen anchor on top of either of the two uprisings and begin
chumming with dead hogmouth fry, small baitfish captured with a cast net
before leaving Bermuda's shores. Various species large and small are attracted
close behind the boat not long after the dead fry are thrown on the surface.

Casts are usually less than 25 feet from the boat transom. Numerous
world-record tuna, wahoo, and other species have been caught from these rich
waters. On my second visit to Bermuda, we had a bumpy 7-mile ride on a
choppy sea running to Challenger Bank. Yet once we were anchored and the

chum dispersed overboard, within minutes we were catching half a dozen varieties of fish. This action continued for more than two hours.

Then a school of fish averaging maybe 1 to 3 pounds swarmed in, taking the hogmouth fry almost as soon as they hit the surface. For me it was a new species, and I always enjoy catching a new species. The fish appeared to be almost round or oval in shape and gray or blue in color. I immediately put on a small Deceiver imitating the hogmouth fry—but the fish ignored it. I tried several other patterns, but they were all rejected. While there were other larger fish in the chum line, I wanted to catch one of these blue-gray devils.

The mate had been watching me with amusement and finally said, "Lefty, they are Bermuda chubs and are damned bait stealers. They have a tiny mouth and are tough to catch with a fly."

I started downsizing my flies. Finally I found a little size 6 bonefish fly. Tying it on, I made a cast and allowed it to sink in front of half a dozen of the chubs. One immediately seized it. I was surprised that such a fish, only 2 pounds, could fight that hard, but I finally landed it. After half a dozen more casts, I caught another. Satisfied, I clipped the tiny bonefish fly from my leader and went back to catching bigger stuff. But I have to admit that for a fish feeding greedily in a chum line it was one of the most difficult to catch.

# Stingray

85

*Rhinoptera bonasus,*
Atlantic stingray, cownose ray

My favorite fishing buddy has always been my son Larry, and we have spent hundreds of hours fly fishing. When he was 12 years old he could throw 80 feet of fly line and loved the sport. Lucky for me one of his favorite pastimes when we lived in Florida was to pole the boat while I stood on the platform and tried for bonefish, redfish, snook, tarpon, and other species.

Flamingo is a National Park operation deep in the Everglades that sits on the west shore of Florida Bay. The water is shallow and richly covered in turtle grass. The grass is perfect habitat for shrimp, crabs, and a variety of baitfish. All of this attracts redfish, snook, and other species. Larry and I spent hundreds of pleasant hours on Flamingo's flats.

One of the things we most enjoyed was fishing muddying rays. These flats teemed with stingrays. Stingrays are not true fish. They have a wide flat body somewhat like the Delta wing of an airplane. Those we sought had mouths located well forward but on the underside of the body.

The bottom of Florida Bay near Flamingo is said to be nearly 30 feet of soft mud covered in rich aquatic grasses. When not feeding, the stingrays sink to the shallow bottom and pound their wings in the mud, creating a cloud of sediment. When the sediment settles, it covers and hides the ray. With the eyes on top of their heads, they can see but are almost impossible to locate.

When the stingrays fed, Larry and I would have fun. It was one of our most enjoyable fly-fishing sports. We would pole along until we found a ray pounding the bottom and stirring up a dense cloud of mud. The ray's object was to pound the bottom with its powerful wings. Any shrimp, crabs, or other creatures disturbed by the mud tried to escape, but many were unfortunate and were captured and eaten by the ray.

Redfish, snook, snappers, jacks, and other species would hover over the muddying ray. They were much swifter than the ray, so when prey tried to escape, the faster-moving fish would swoop in and grab it before the ray could.

There were times when almost every mudding ray would have one or more fish hovering above it ready to pounce on what it disturbed. Such fish were in a feeding mood, and a fly placed properly at the forward end of the mud resulted in a hookup. It was like a lottery—you never knew which species would be on the next ray.

One pleasant afternoon Larry was poling toward another mudding ray. Once in position I cast a fly into the mud and started a retrieve and was immediately hooked to something powerful. It was soon evident I had hooked the ray. It sped across the flat leaving behind a wide mud trail. Soon backing appeared, and I urged Larry to pole faster to keep up. The mud was so soft that Larry simply couldn't maintain enough boat speed. I realized I was going to lose leader, fly line, and backing, so as the spool diminished I clamped on the reel and broke the leader.

We both sat down and began to laugh. Talking about it we realized what happened was a good thing. Those rays carry a venomous stinger in the tail, and had we gotten it to the boat we would have been in a dilemma as to how to land and release it. But I shall not forget the power of that ray as it towed my fly and line across the flats when escaping.

# Boxfish

**86**

## Family Ostraciidae

O f all species I've caught on a fly rod, the bonefish is my favorite. And to catch them tailing is even more fun. A tailing bonefish in the shallows often tilts its head down, sucking in a shrimp, crab, or other morsel hidden just under the film of dirt or sand on the bottom. It can detect a snapping shrimp or crab hiding just under that film. The bonefish opens its mouth, sucking sand, dirt, and the creature, and then expelling dirt and sand out the gills. An experienced bonefisherman poling a flat will recognize where bonefish have recently captured prey by the newly disturbed small craters and will even know the direction the fish had been swimming.

When the bonefish is tailing, the head is down and the tail is above water waving much like a small silver flag would in the breeze.

The boxfish tails too but in a different manner, and once you see it, it is easy to recognize. The small tail extends above the surface and rapidly beats back and forth with regularity. Bonefish are often difficult to see on a flat, but boxfish are not.

**172**

I decided to catch one, and my guide suggested using a size 6 bonefish fly. The guide approached the boxfish with its head down and tail up busy worrying something on the bottom. I cast the fly about a foot in front of the fish and slow-stripped the retrieve. The boxfish jumped on it. I must say the fight was disappointing; minutes later the guide reached down, picked it up, and placed it on the bow.

I reached for my camera because this was one of the most unusual fish I'd seen. Now I understood why they call it a boxfish. The fish was encased in an almost square bony exterior and because of it the fish couldn't move. I picked it up and tried to squeeze it—the hard shell was unyielding.

The guide said they are good to eat. I think he said they bake them and then break open the bony shell to get at the tasty flesh. After a few photos I put it back in the water.

# Cutlassfish

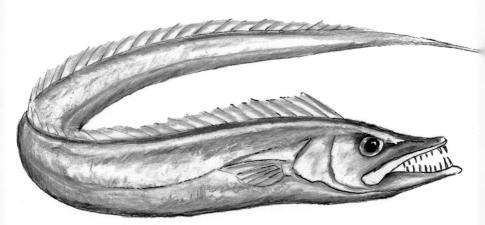

## 87

## Family Trichiuridae, ribbonfish

I was fishing with one of my best friends, Bob Clouser, the man who gave fly fishermen the Clouser Minnow. We were staying at Casa Mar, the famous jungle tarpon camp in northeastern Costa Rica. Near the lodge ran the Rio Colorado, a big and always muddy river where hundreds of tarpon have been caught on flies before the river enters the Atlantic Ocean.

There is a plume of dirty river water that extends some distance out from the mouth of the river into the clear waters of the Atlantic. Sea water is heavier than fresh water, and divers told me that if you swim down through the muddy river water, below the sea is clear and big tarpon often rest there like people seeking comfortable shade from the bright sun.

Using lead-core shooting heads, many of us braved the turbulent waters at the river's mouth to get outside and then fish for tarpon either below the muddy plume or near where the tarpon were rolling on the surface.

During one retrieve I felt a light tap and set the hook. There was so little resistance I knew it wasn't a tarpon—not even a small one. It was quickly brought boatside, and Bob and I could not believe it. It was a cutlassfish, often called a ribbonfish.

It doesn't look like a fish and is one of the most unusual you'll ever see. Its 3-foot-long, eel-like body was bright shiny silver and reflected sunlight when brought aboard. What really set it apart, though, was the mouth. Its large open jaws snapped as it lay on the bottom of the boat, and the mouth was filled with fang-like teeth, making it look formidable. It's like a flat-bodied eel with a dragon's head. Carefully Bob held it up, and I took several photos. We released it, and I have never caught another—nor do I want to.

# Pompano

## 88

*Trachinotus carolinus,*
Florida pompano

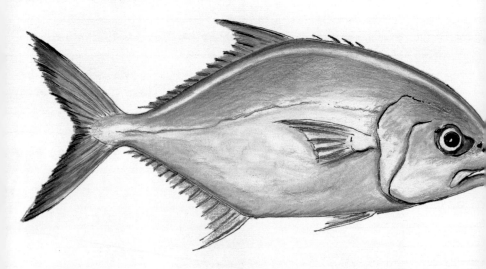

For several years in the late 1960s and early 1970s, I was fortunate to be a guest of the Bermuda Fishing Tourist Agency with a mission to fish these fabled waters and write about them. While I did catch a few fish inshore, there are limited shallows surrounding the island. Most of the fly fishing was in the deep Atlantic Ocean and on the Challenger and Argus banks that rose from the sea floor close to the surface, where fishing was fantastic.

My good friend Pete Perinchief was charged with managing the fishing tourist business. Pete was a top-flight angler with fly, plug, or spinning tackle and also one of the most informed fishermen I ever met about tying superior knots.

For several days at Challenger Bank we had caught a number of species of fish and many of them. We were having a wonderful breakfast at Cambridge Beaches, one of Bermuda's finest luxury resorts. As we finished our coffee

Pete asked, "We can go offshore again or wade one of our flats, but I would like to take you for pompano. Are you interested?"    ·

Of course I was, but my experience at catching pompano with a fly had usually ended in failure. Pete said, "I'll bring the tackle, but we will fish in the surf, so wear wading shoes and an old pair of pants."

Pompano I think are in the jack family, but they are small, usually 1 or 2 pounds. They tend to travel in schools and you can often find them close to or in the surf searching for sand fleas, one of their favorite foods. Just about everyone agrees they are among the most delicious fish in the sea.

Pete stopped at the local store and bought a loaf of bread, which I thought was for our lunch. We rigged the two 6-weight fly rods with floating line and a 7-foot leader tapered to a tippet that appeared to be 4-pound-test. The location Pete picked was a small cove where the beach dropped off sharply. Opening the bread, he began tearing it into small pieces and with my help threw it into the surf. "Be patient, and we'll have some fun," Pete predicted. After perhaps 20 minutes, I began to see silver flashes under the water where obviously something was taking the bread.

Among Pete's many accomplishments, he was a fine fly tier. "Tie this on and cast it out and let it settle near the bread and don't retrieve it." he instructed. The fly had a bit of white deer hair spun on the size 6 hook with two wraps of short white marabou near the hook eye.

I did as he asked, and as the fly sunk below the waves a silver streak swept in and inhaled it. I was fast to a 2-pound pompano on a 6-weight rod. Remember, they are in the jack family, so it took me some time to finally land it. Pete picked it up, removed the hook, and dropped it in his cooler. "We will keep some for dinner," he explained.

We spent the morning in that cove catching pompano until we ran out of bread. It was great fun, but what really topped it off was the dinner. I don't know how the chef did it, but he brought us each pompano that had been cooked in brown paper bags. Why the bags never caught fire during cooking, I don't know, but it was one of the tastiest dinners I had in a long time.

# Tripletail

**89**

*Lobotes surinamensis*,
leaf fish, drift fish, buoy bass, triplefin

The tripletail is so named because the anal, dorsal, and caudal fins sweep back from the body, forming what looks like three tails. While they are supposedly found in a number of places, the only ones I've seen were on the west coast of Florida. The tripletail has small eyes but a large mouth, and the front of the fish is almost triangular.

Adults are usually caught weighing 4 to 10 pounds but get much larger. The have a strange habit of floating motionless on their sides near the surface—much like floating debris—and then ambushing small prey as it swims by. They are frequently found around channel buoys, saragassum algae, or any floating object, whether a cooler top that blew off someone's boat, a log, a board, or just about anything that floats.

Tripletail are one of the better-eating fish in the sea and highly prized. I think Florida now has a strict limit on how many can be kept simply because they were being overharvested.

I recall how years ago they saved for us from what appeared to be a poor fishing outing. Tarpon fishing had been excellent, so three of us put in at Boca Grande, Florida, and spent several hours looking for them. We found one small pod that had obviously been spooked because they were swimming fast to get out of the area.

Late in the afternoon one of us remarked, "This tarpon fishing sucks; why not try for some tripletail?" We had 8-weight rods aboard, so we rigged them with small minnow imitation patterns and headed for some buoys nearby. There was nothing on the first buoy but two tripletails on the next—both fish took our flies. They are strong fighters and strained our 8-weights.

We began cruising and looking for any floating objects. Over the next two hours we found several and landed three more. What had been a lousy tarpon day turned out to be a winner when we forgot tarpon and went after tripletails.

# Fallfish

## 90

*Semotilus corporalis*

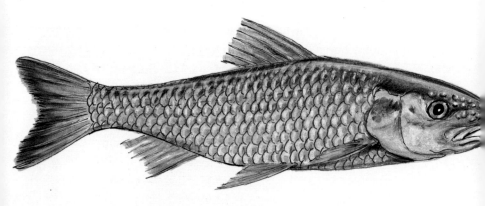

I was born in central Maryland in a small town of maybe 12,000 called Frederick. Today it is the second-largest city in the state, but when I was growing up I could walk half a mile out of town to fish local limestone streams or the Monocacy River. Within half an hour's drive was the Potomac River. A 5-mile walk away were the Blue Ridge Mountains, which held brook trout and a few browns. The coveted gamefish most anglers sought was the smallmouth bass, and they were commonly caught to 4 pounds—and lots of them.

In my youth I enjoyed hanging around the old-timers who chatted about their younger days. Often without realizing it, they gave me tips on how, when, or where to fish or hunt. One of the things I found enchanting was that these old-timers said their grandfathers told them there were almost no smallmouth bass in the local streams during their time. Instead their favorite gamefish was the fallfish.

The fallfish reminds me of a large chub coated in silvery scales. It lives in relatively small streams or rivers the size of the Potomac. It feeds on the same things as the smallmouth bass, but apparently the smallmouth is more aggressive. As I understand it, the smallmouth was introduced in the late 1880s into the big limestone rivers of the mid-Atlantic region via the railroad. Train locomotives carried a lot of water to generate steam. Smallmouth bass from Ohio were transported in the train's water tanks and stocked in these rivers. The rivers were rich in crayfish, minnows, and hellgrammites, and the bass flourished. Within a few decades, they had become the major predator fish, and the fallfish apparently couldn't compete, so they began disappearing.

I began to seriously fly-fish my local rivers and streams in the early 1950s, and there were still enough fallfish around that you caught a few, especially in the smaller meadow streams we waded. Most fallfish were 6 to maybe 10 or 12 inches.

I used a 13-foot Grumman canoe extensively to fish our rivers. The Monocacy River averaged about 75 to 100 yards wide and at the time held many deep pools. Fallfish and smallmouth eagerly strike popping bugs. One day below Creagerstown, Maryland, on the Monocacy I cast my popper to a limestone ledge in deep water, and the moment it landed it was sucked under. I struck and a large silvery fish leaped into the air. I thought it might be a shad.

It put up a fair fight, and after the first jump I realized it was a fallfish. Having caught hundreds of them, I was stunned at the size of this one and didn't want to lose it. My companion and great friend, Flip Kennedy, worked the canoe to shallow water, and I got out. I was able to lift the fish from the water. It was 18 inches long and heavy in the body. Our scales were never accurate, but it pulled it down to almost 4 pounds. Neither Flip nor I have ever seen a fallfish this large—before or since. For me it was a banner day.

# Mutton Snapper

91

*Lutjanus analis*,
muttonfish

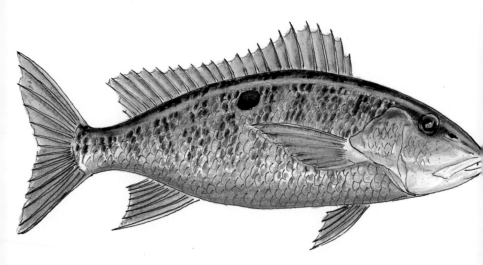

S ome experienced flats fly fishermen have the opinion (as do I) that the mutton snapper is harder to catch on a fly than the wily permit. I have caught thousands of fish on flies, but I regard an 18-pound mutton snapper as one of my luckiest and best catches.

Mutton snapper are among the prettiest of all the snapper family. The back is olive in color with rose or pink sides, a white belly, and a round black spot near the dorsal fin. Most are found in deep water, but they do sometimes come up on the flats where they are spookier than a cat in a dog pound.

In the 1960s and '70s, muttons often were found on the shallow flats in the lower Florida Keys. If you located a free-swimming mutton, it would flee or often refuse to take your offering. But muttons have a habit of following a ray as its swims across the flats. Should the ray spook something, the swifter mutton will beat the ray to it. If a ray begins to pound on the bottom to flush food and a mutton hovers over, it becomes intent on feeding and seems to lose much of its natural caution. This situation offers the best opportunity for fly fishermen, and that was how I managed to catch that 18-pounder.

When commercial fishermen began setting wire mesh traps on the Florida Keys reefs in the mid-1970s, a serious decline occurred in muttons. Today it is rare to find one.

A few years ago I fished again in Cuba in the Garden of the Queens, a spot 50 miles offshore from the mainland. Castro had created a large marine preserve there where no commercial fishing has been allowed for years. We stayed aboard the Avalon Company barge with a number of other fly fishermen, and we fished flats that had not been disturbed by anglers for decades.

While we had a fantastic time catching many fish, the highlight for me was catching five mutton snappers on the flats on flies. I won't tell you how many I cast to—but those five made my week.

# Chum Salmon

# 92

*Oncorhynchus keta,*
chum, dog salmon

The chum salmon, often called dog salmon in the Bristol Bay area of Alaska, usually enter the watersheds just after the king salmon spawn. They are an attractive fish with pronounced markings on their sides during the spawning stage. These markings are unlike any of the other four Pacific species of salmon. They are the only species to regain their parr marks, which are the marks displayed by baby salmon. Chum salmon average from about 5 to 15 pounds and put up a good account when hooked. Some people say king and silver salmons have a better taste, but Eskimos I have talked to think chum salmon are delicious. They catch, fillet, and air-dry them for winter food.

Chums take flies readily, and I recall once on the Rainbow River when I caught about 38 chums on about 40 casts. They can be in such dense schools that I often use the weedless-style bendback flies to prevent snagging them because a conventional hook often hooks them in the back or side.

I can remember many wonderful days fishing for chums, but one stands out above the others. We were fishing from a gravel bar and casting to a deeper pool on the far side. Along the other side of the river was a worn bear path. Walking down it came a huge Kodiak bear, acting strange. The bear peered into the water and stood on three feet, the right forward leg upraised and poised to strike. Suddenly it slashed down with the leg and threw a chum salmon on the bank and then sat and ate it. The bear moved a few yards downriver and repeated the motion. Apparently the bear didn't want to get wet. That seemed strange since every bear I had seen chased salmon by jumping in the water, often immersing itself completely to grab salmon. We watched that finicky bear catch more than a dozen salmon using just his one paw as he moved downriver and around the bend.

# Goliath Grouper 93

*Epinephelus itajara,*
jewfish

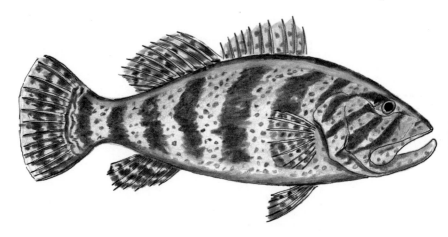

The goliath grouper for decades was called the jewfish, and I am not sure why it was renamed. Most people in Florida still call it the jewfish, and I will do so here—hoping none of my good Jewish friends are offended.

This fish can reach enormous size and is believed to grow to at least 800 pounds. While I was at the *Miami Herald* in the late 1960s a scuba diver swimming near a Gulf of Mexico wreck reported that a jewfish tried to inhale him. The man said his head and half his body was sucked inside the grouper. He used his elbows and pounded against the fish's gills until it expelled him. The report said pronounced bruises were visible on his body, and the diver estimated that the jewfish might have weighed 1,000 pounds.

Jewfish are good to eat, and so many were caught and kept that some years ago Florida banned anglers from keeping them. At this writing fishermen are complaining that there are too many jewfish because of the ban. The complaint is that jewfish often live in or near wrecks. When fishermen try landing other species, these giant jewfish easily catch and eat the angler's struggling fish. This is happening so often that wreck fishing is becoming a waste of time.

Before the ban began we used to fly-fish the flats for "baby" jewfish—those weighing from 10 to 35 or so pounds. These fish were often in less than 4 feet of water on the flats and almost always were under a log, tree stump, or old limbs. It was easy to locate them. We would cruise the flats and check each of these structures. If a jewfish was living under one, the normally dark bottom would show bright yellow where the fish had disturbed the bottom when moving its tail and fins while at rest. They eagerly accepted large Deceiver flies. If we could keep the powerful fish from the structure, we could catch and release them. It was great fun, and I miss that sport.

But my favorite story about jewfish is not about one I caught but something that happened to Dan Schooler, a good friend of mine. Dan was the greatest practical joker I ever knew, and no one was immune to his tricks. All of us watched him like a hawk checking out a mouse. Dan's greatest pleasure was to play the joke and then tell everyone about it. The best part of this story is that while he pulled off the joke, it backfired on him.

Dan had a business in Miami, and a business associate from New York City came for a visit and asked Dan to take him fishing. Wanting to be in the man's good graces, Dan, a superb fisherman, assured the man he would have a good time and catch fish.

The day before their trip, Dan and a friend went fishing, and Dan caught a nice jewfish of maybe 40 pounds. Since Dan ate almost anything he caught, he had a large live well in his boat. On a whim he put the jewfish in the live well. The man met Dan at the dock the next morning, and they took off.

According to Dan, the man was totally inept as a fisherman. The few fish he hooked he lost. By midday the New Yorker was bored with the whole thing and fell asleep. Desperate for the man to have good fishing day, Dan suddenly remembered the big jewfish in his boat. While the man was asleep, Dan carefully lifted his line from the water and quietly impaled the big jewfish on the man's hook and lowered it into the water.

Dan sat back and the jewfish soon recovered and began swimming away. The man's rod bent, and Dan yelled to the man he had hooked a fish. Instantly the man went into action and a hard battle ensured. Dan finally was able to net the fish. The man was stunned—he had never caught anything so large and wanted pictures. And then he told Dan he wanted it mounted so he could display it in his New York office. Of course Dan had to do as he wished.

Dan was so tickled he had pulled off his joke, but what was devastating to him was that because this man was an important client he was afraid to tell anyone but two or three of his closest friends and swore us to secrecy.

# King Mackerel 94

*Scomberomorus cavalla,*
king, kingfish, giant mackerel

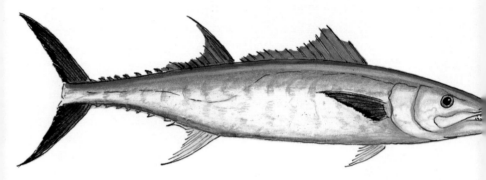

O ne of the most exciting inshore fish you can catch with fly tackle is a king mackerel, sometimes confused with wahoo. It does not have the dark vertical bars of the wahoo, though, which pretty much disappear when the fish dies. The sure way to tell which is which is after death: the wahoo has a thin lateral line running straight from just behind the gill flap to the tail, while the king mackerel has a similar thin lateral line that starts straight, high on the body, angles downward about midbody, and then runs straight toward the tail. The wahoo has a reputation of being one of the fastest fish in the sea and a great fighter when hooked with fly or light tackle. I think it is difficult to tell the difference between the two species when you hook a large one.

King mackerel are usually caught in the 5- to 30-pound size, but giants get to 80 or 90 pounds. They are a long, sleek fish that strike with the speed of a barracuda. They are usually found in the inshore waters. They are such prized gamefish that a number of fishing tournaments are geared around just catching them.

I think the most spectacular thing about king mackerel is their ability to shoot from the water in a high leap before falling back into the sea. The mackerel find a school of baitfish and swim below them, pushing them toward the surface. The long, narrow fish can't turn quickly when chasing prey. Instead they concentrate on a target and then launch like a rocket in a straight line. Many times they travel so fast as they shoot up toward the bait near the surface they leap high above the water before dropping back.

Smith Shoal Light, about 8 miles from Key West, for many years would see a winter run of king mackerel, which may still be true. Between the Smith light and Edmund Lowe Shoals to the east is an underwater ridge where baitfish tended to congregate, luring king mackerel. It was one of the best places I knew to try for kings on a fly rod.

You'd carry baitfish in the live well and anchor where the kings were active. Every now and then you would throw a baitfish near the boat, and soon a few kings would show. We would stun the baitfish before throwing them overboard so they either would lie motionless in the water or move little. As soon as the kings would show, we would toss a stunned baitfish and cast a Deceiver fly near it but not retrieve it. It worked—we caught a number of kings that took the baitfish and the fly.

I had a 16-foot Starcraft aluminum boat, and on calm days I would make the run out there—keeping an eye on the weather because the boat was not designed to run there when the gulf got rough. My most memorable moment was one day when I hooked a king mackerel of maybe 30 pounds that took the fly within a few yards of the boat. But it came from below and rocketed into the air. I yelled and we ducked and the fish leaped so high it rainbowed over the boat, falling in the water on the other side—snapping my leader. But I didn't care. What a treat it was to see that fish make that overhead leap.

# Cutthroat Trout 95

*Oncorhynchus clarkii,*
cutties, cutts

For many years I would spend part of my summer trout fishing out west. Gradually my favorite destination became West Yellowstone. From this base you can fish hidden mountain lakes, a dozen large and small rivers, Henry's Fork, Quake Lake, the Madison and Gallatin rivers, and all the waters in Yellowstone Park, whose entrance was hundreds of yards from the town.

My first year there I caught a number of good rainbows and brown trout, but I wanted to catch a Montana cutthroat trout. They are small fish, averaging usually 10 to 14 inches and sometimes a little larger. Size didn't matter, I just had a hankering to catch one.

Arriving in West Yellowstone just out of the park, we drove to Reds Davis, who in the 1960s had a number of rental cabins where I always stayed when in the town. Reds was a tall lanky guy who taught me (I'm 5 foot, 7 inches) never to wade where such a tall guy does—my waders are not as high. I had fished several years with Reds, and we became fast friends. I told him I had caught lots of rainbows and browns in local rivers and lakes but really wanted to catch a Montana cutthroat trout. Reds explained they never get very large, but if I was willing he'd take me to them.

Entering Yellowstone Park, Reds drove for miles on hard roads and then on to a little-used, rough dirt road where his four-wheel-drive Suburban had no problem. We bounced along until we came to a small lake with a stream leaving it that was no more than 20 feet wide. Getting out, Reds handed me a 4-weight rod with a small dry fly attached to the 7½-foot leader. Reds said, "Work those riffles, and you'll catch a bunch of those cutthroats."

On the second cast a small trout grabbed the fly and I landed it. It was a Montana cutthroat, a beautiful fish with a light tan greenish back full of spots, a rose-colored cheek with the typical red cutthroat slash on the lower jaw, and an orange belly. I gently put it back.

A few minutes later I landed my second Montana cutthroat, maybe a foot in length. Reds explained, "That's a big one, and you probably won't catch one larger." I waded to shore, thanking Reds for this opportunity. We returned to the hard road and stopped at the Madison River on the way home, catching a few browns much larger. No matter, I thanked Reds for catching a species that had never fallen to my fly rod before.

When I think of cutthroat trout I instantly recall another experience on that trip with my fishing buddy Leon Martuch Jr., who ran Scientific Anglers. The chief ranger offered to give us a tour of Yellowstone, and we jumped at the chance.

We had been driving for maybe an hour, enjoying what has to be our most beautiful and unusual national park, when we saw a traffic jam ahead. Our ranger friend said, "Oh my, we've run into a bear-a-cade." Cars had stopped and people were out of their cars taking photos within yards of a black bear. The ranger had a loudspeaker on top of the car, and he announced, "Please don't get close to the bear; please move on." After several such announcements and people ignoring him, he turned on his siren, and when it began wailing, that bear left in hurry. People got in their cars and moved on.

Later that day we were driving along the road where an open field lay on our right with a mountain beyond. As we got close to a traffic jam we saw no bear and wondered what was drawing all the peoples' attention. At the far side of the field just outside the wooded hill stood a full-grown mountain lion looking at us. I had my camera with a long telephoto lens, and as I focused on the lion, I heard people screaming in terror. Through the lens, I saw two young men running down two paths that would bring them too close to the lion. People were yelling at the two men, but they kept rushing forward. I was looking at this though my lens and figured I was going to get one helluva shot. The two young men emerged from the woods, ran forward, picked up the stuffed animal, and carried it back in the woods. They had pulled a joke on everyone. There was instant relief, then some laughter, and a few were cussing, but it was one of the best practical jokes I ever saw.

# Fingermark Bream

# 96

*Lutjanus johnii,*
fingermark, spotted-scale sea perch,
golden snapper, red chopper

This is a pretty fish we caught in New Guinea, although they are found in warmer northern Australian waters too. They get their name from a distinct thumbprint-like black spot found near the tail. The natives in New Guinea said they call it a fingermark bream because the very outer edge of each of the scales has a faint dark line—similar to the appearance of dirt under the fingernails. The body is a soft pink color. They can grow to more than 20 pounds and are shaped like the snappers we find on Florida's reefs. They are delicious and are in the same *Lutjanus* genus as the cubera snapper, so they are strong fighters when hooked.

We were in New Guinea making a TV show for an Australian firm and living in a thatched house constructed by natives the week before. The male natives had bones in their noses and carried bows and arrows and spears and the women had used seashells to cut designs in their breasts and faces and then rubbed ashes in the wounds to appear attractive. I thought that made them so ugly they would bring tears to a glass eyeball—but the native men apparently liked them.

Fingermark bream are often found on reefs and around wrecks. Because they are so good to eat, Australia has daily limits to prevent overharvesting. Stout tackle is used to prevent the strong fish from getting back to the deeper reefs or wrecks and cutting the anglers' lines.

The camera crew was able to get good footage for the TV show of Rod Harrison, Australia's senior fishing writer and me, so Rod suggested trying for fingermark bream for a delicious dinner. I had expected we would go to a reef outside of the Kulu River where we had been filming. Instead we motored several hundred yards out the river mouth and anchored in maybe 15 to 18 feet of water.

Rod suggested I rig a 9-weight fly rod with a fast sinking line and a 3- or 4-inch Deceiver fly. Rod tied a white jig on his plug-fishing outfit and made a cast. Within a few minutes he was hooked to a fingermark bream. Two others in the boat using the same tackle began hooking fingermarks. As they brought their fish near the boat the water turned pink as scores of the fingermarks rose with their hooked companions. I dropped my fly among them and was immediately fighting a strong bream. We kept enough for dinner but caught and released a great many more.

I shall never forget standing in the boat and casting to so many fingermark bream within 20 feet of the boat that they turned the water light pink.

# Whitetip Shark 97

*Triaenoden obesus,*
reef shark

Christmas Island is so named because Captain Cook discovered it on Christmas day. It's the largest atoll—a coral reef surrounding a lagoon—in the world at 60 miles around and is located about 1,200 miles south of Hawaii in the vast Pacific Ocean. Christmas Island has one opening that allows the tide to flow in and out of the huge lagoon. That lagoon is filled with shallow flats dissected by channels. It is one of the top destinations in the world to fly-fish for bonefish, and thousands of anglers have visited it.

Over the years I was fortunate to take a number of fly-fishing groups to Christmas Island, which has some of the best wading flats anywhere. It is not unusual for an experienced bonefisherman to catch 20 or more fish a day. On perhaps my fourth or fifth trip there I received a very unpleasant surprise.

Many whitetip sharks cruise these flats looking for crippled bonefish and other prey. They are incredibly swift when pursuing something. On several occasions when a bonefish was hooked and ran a considerable distance, these whitetips would dart in and grab the fish.

Wading with one of my clients, I hooked a bonefish of maybe 3 pounds. It ran off a short distance, and I began to wind it closer. Suddenly a whitetip began pursuing it. I tried to break the leader tippet to give the bonefish a chance to escape, but the bone was streaking directly at me, creating slack line. Before I knew it, the bonefish was several yards from my feet with the whitetip in hot pursuit. I slapped the rod down on the water to discourage the shark— no luck. When the bonefish was within 4 feet of me, the shark swooped in and grabbed the bone. I admit it scared the hell out of me and there was blood in the water around my legs—at least I think it was all blood!

# Remora

## 98

*Remora* sp.,
sharksucker, suckerfish

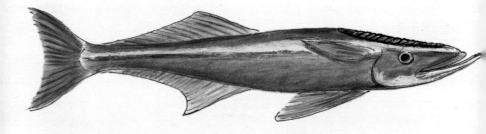

I was fly fishing with famed local angler Norm Jansik, a close friend, out of Flamingo in Everglades National Park. These flats are rich with many fish species and the foods they eat.

We saw an unusually large ray creating a wide mud streak. We were sure that a fast-swimming snapper, jack, or redfish would be hovering above the ray ready to pounce on what the ray flushed from the bottom. Norm poled the boat close. I made a cast where the mud was most dense, and began a retrieve, when something grabbed it immediately. It wasn't a jack crevalle but put up a better fight than a snapper or redfish. It was too dark to be either, and it stayed within the cloud of mud trailing downcurrent behind the ray.

Norm backed the boat away and with the rod side pressure pulled the thing out of the mud streak, and we were astonished. It was the biggest remora that either of us had seen. It was almost 3 feet long!

The remora is an unusual fish that has a row of suckers on the flat portion of the body directly above the eyes. It attaches to larger fish and is towed along as the larger one swims. The bigger fish attacks prey, and when any tidbits fall from the prey, the remora leaves the host fish and grabs them. I've also seen remoras act like the cattle egrets that walk beside cattle grabbing the insects stirred by the cattle hooves.

Norm and I've caught a number of remoras, but never one this size. And we had never seen a remora feeding over a mudding ray.

# Spanish Mackerel

# 99

## *Scomberomorus maculatus*

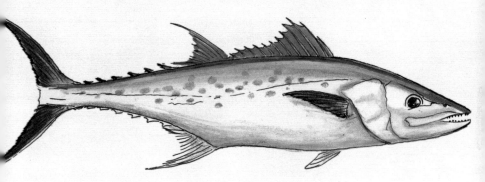

Spanish mackerel (the Atlantic species) look like small king mackerel and are just as voracious. They have teeth similar to bluefish, and they travel in schools—often large schools. They chase the bait to the surface and slash into them, and once you see a school working bait they are easily to identify.

A big Spanish might be 2 feet long, although most are from 14 to 18 inches. They have a tuna-shaped sickle tail and are built for speed and endurance. Their favorite food seems to be small baitfish, so small flies are the ticket. Because of those sharp teeth, we usually use 30- or even 40-pound-test fluorocarbon or very thin flexible wire attached to the fly. The mackerels' eyesight is incredible.

Most anglers visit South Florida to fly-fish for giant tarpon, permit, bonefish, and redfish. But those of us who lived there also enjoy using light fly rods to chase a number of other species often ignored by visiting anglers.

I can attest you can't have more fun with a 6-weight rod and floating line with a small streamer fly than when chasing schools of hungry Spanish mackerel, catching one after another.

# Yellow Perch 100

*Perca flavescens,*
lake perch, American perch, ringed perch,
striped perch, jack perch

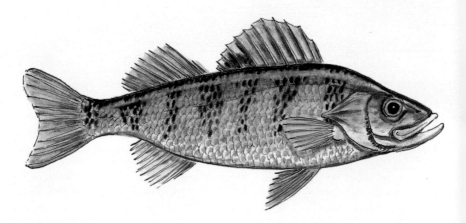

I n Maryland where I've lived most of my life, the first native species to run the rivers and creeks to spawn is the yellow perch, and it can be as early as late February. At this time you are ready to catch anything on a fly rod after being trapped inside all winter tying flies, reading about fly fishing, or looking at some lucky guys on TV having fun in tropical waters. The yellow perch was the answer.

Yellow perch are widely distributed, and I have caught them in remote Canadian lakes near the Arctic Circle and in warm ponds in South Carolina. They get their name from their greenish yellow or gold bodies that have pronounced vertical bars. The meat is delicious, and my favorite cooking method is to make filleted fingers dipped in beer batter and deep-fried.

A big yellow perch may only be 10 or 12 inches. When yellow perch are spawning you can't miss their egg cases in large gelatinous strands, which are strewn over the bottom and draped among sunken limbs.

During the 1970s, one of my best friends, outdoor writer Boyd Pfeiffer, and his son Jeff and my son Larry and I journeyed to the Eastern Shore of

Maryland to fish for yellow perch. We started the two-hour drive before dawn. A 15-foot aluminum canoe sat atop my sedan and Boyd's van carried a 14-foot johnboat. The drive over was peaceful and the wind calm.

Boyd and I were intimately familiar with the local small streams we planned to fish for spawning yellow perch, and during the morning all four of us had a great time. About noon we pulled into a dirt parking area near a small stream, and we noticed the wind had picked up considerably. The sky was clear, but the wind was at least 25 mph. Since we were sheltered by thick woods, we thought nothing of it and began catching a few perch.

The wind began intensifying and within half an hour it was howling. Boyd and I became concerned, and we were convinced to get out of there when several tall dead trees were blown over, crashing to the forest floor.

As we drove north on the Eastern Shore, our radios began telling about the freak wind that was now more than 50 mph. As we neared the Chesapeake Bay Bridge to leave the Eastern Shore of Maryland and cross to the Western Shore, we heard reports of several tractor trailers blown over on roads.

To get home we had to cross the Chesapeake Bay Bridge, which is more than 4 miles long. But in the middle it rises hundreds of feet above the water to allow large ships going to Baltimore Harbor to pass below. As we approached the bridge, Larry was driving our car, and we could feel the wind pushing against the car and canoe. In the rearview mirror I could see the wind blowing against Boyd's van with the even larger johnboat on top.

The bridge on either end is just a few yards above Chesapeake Bay, but it rises steadily toward the middle. As both vehicles began the climb, we could feel them being pushed sideways. Larry and Boyd were doing a great job of controlling the vehicles, but they soon began driving in the upwind lane in case the wind blew us too far to the side. Nearing the top of the bridge, we really felt the force of the wind, and Boyd and Larry struggled to keep us on the bridge. Looking over, I could see that the only thing keeping us on the road if blown sideways was what appeared to be thin steel railings.

I have to admit I was scared, and neither of us talked. I didn't want to spoil Larry's driving concentration, and he was focusing on keeping us on the bridge. As we neared the lower western end of the bridge the wind's effect reduced, and I left out a sigh. I had been so tense I thought I was going to get rope burns on my hands I was saying my Rosary so fast. Once we were off the bridge, the wind still was a problem, but the ride home was nothing compared to being hundreds of feet above the water on the bridge. When winds get to 50 mph today, they close the bridge to traffic. When I think of yellow perch I often think of that harrowing ride across the bridge.

# Permit

*Trachinotus*

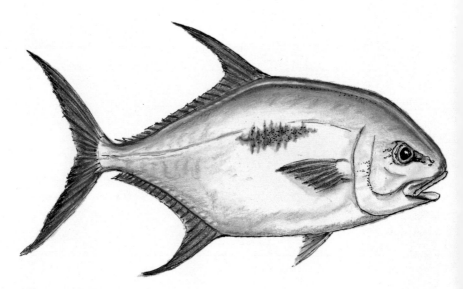

I caught my first permit on a fly and knew it was a fluke. In the late 1960s, outdoor writer Mark Sosin was poling me along the north side of the Marquesas, a string of mangrove islands 25 miles west of Key West. We saw a school of small permit swimming along the shoreline, and I threw a bonefish fly into the school and hooked and landed a permit of maybe 16 inches. I was so delighted that Mark took a photo of me kissing it—the only time my lips ever touched a live fish. It was a number of years before I caught my next permit.

I first met Del Brown in Alaska many years ago—I think in the late 1970s. After fishing with him one day, I knew he and I would get along great. Over the years we fished in a number of places: New Zealand, South America, Central America, and the United States. We became close friends.

Del Brown was not a world-record seeker, but not too many years ago, he set for himself a personal goal of catching 500 permit on a fly. He was well on his way to succeeding when in one of our frequent phone conversations I asked if I could spend time with him in the boat with one of his all-time favorite guides, Capt. Steve Huff. I insisted I did not want to fish but take photos and learn his tricks for catching the wily permit, which many fly fishermen agree is the ultimate flats trophy. He was delighted, and I shared Steve's skiff with him a number of days. It was like getting a master's degree in permit fishing. Those wonderful days paid off for me. With friends or guides, I had caught several permit, but none were unusually large, most in the 10- to maybe 15-pound size. Still, they were permit, and I was happy.

When Castro took over Cuba in 1959, Joe Brooks was hired to help promote sport fishing there to develop income for the country. He invited me, along with several other outdoor writers, and I was lucky enough to spend 18 days there immediately after the revolution. I was amazed at the fantastic flats fishing.

In June of 2005 I was invited to return as a guest of Avalon Cuban Fishing Centers, an Italian company that had a fishing lodge and barge in the Garden of the Queens, a 100-mile string of mangrove and sandy islands 50 miles south of Cuba. Soon after Castro took over, he declared the Garden of the Queens a marine preserve and banned commercial fishing there.

Can you imagine a remote, pristine flats wilderness where no one had commercially fished for the last 50 years? The barge accommodated 28 anglers sleeping two to a small room and had a large dining area where they served great meals with the freshest fish you can imagine. I don't smoke or drink, but after dinner Cuban cigars smoked up the room as my friends told great stories of their catches while drinks sweated on the table.

Each morning two fishermen and a guide departed in different directions to fish the vast resource. The fishing was as good as it gets. Bonefish teemed on the flats—bordering the ocean, some flats were a mile long. Only rarely did you see another skiff off in the distance as it raced to another spot. Unfortunately, Avalon was just starting its operation, and many of the guides were not fluent in English—although between us we got the job done. I understand now all guides are fluent in English.

One morning I noticed three empty seats at the breakfast table and was informed three of our party were sick and would not be fishing that day. I was asked if I would mind fishing alone with a young and little-experienced guide who knew the waters well. Of course I was delighted.

The first place we went was a deep narrow channel that held baby tarpon. The guide anchored the boat near a small mangrove island. The high tide was running through the mangrove roots. He dove overboard, swam to the other side of the island, and began wading slowly back to the boat. Suddenly a dozen or more 20-pound tarpon eased out of the mangroves into the channel where I promptly hooked one. One a subsequent trip with my great friend John Zajano, we did this again, and it is a most unusual method of tarpon fishing.

After some discussion, I conveyed to the guide I'd like to catch a permit. His eyes lit up, and I think he was saying, "You bet I know where some are." We made a fairly long run to a flat bordering some deep water. I tied on a Merkin crab pattern, and he began poling. We saw several permit moving so fast we never got a shot at them. Then we were fortunate to see one of the most exciting flats sights—a big permit tailing. Standing almost on its head, it attempted to root out its prey. The head came up, and it started swimming, so I dropped the fly two feet in front of it.

The permit surged forward, and one of the things Del Brown taught me was when a permit tilts downward, begin a slow retrieve, drawing tight on the line. Permit can inhale a fly and eject it so fast that anglers often waiting to feel the fish take the fly don't strike until the fish has spit out the fly. Just as Del predicted, the fish was on, and the outcome was in doubt for at least 15 minutes. Finally the permit was at boatside, and I guessed it at more than 25 pounds. The young guide grabbed it by the tail, and it thrashed back and forth and was torn from his hands, falling back into the water and disappearing. He was mortified, but I didn't care. I had caught my first big permit, and it couldn't have been in a more pristine, beautiful place.